LETTERS ON THE HEALING MINISTRY

LETTERS
ON THE
HEALING MINISTRY

ALBERT E. DAY

Study Guide by James K. Wagner

THE UPPER ROOM
Nashville, Tennessee

Letters on the Healing Ministry

Contents

Introduction

WHEN I FIRST READ THIS UNIQUE BOOK AS AN
investigating, curious, young pastor in the 1960s, I
was impressed by the author's authenticity and
humility. I found his scholarly and pastoral understandings, his genuine desire to share his experiences and continuing research with other
Christians to be very encouraging. I recognized
myself in the pages of these twelve letters "addressed to a minister with a critical intelligence
and with a passionate concern that his ministry to
the people for whom Christ gave his life might be
all that he intended it to be."

Today, more than twenty years after this book's
first printing, the healing ministry of the church is
receiving unprecedented attention. Albert E. Day's
insight needs to be shared with the ever-increasing
numbers of clergy and laity who are bringing their
own critical intelligence and passionate concern to
this fascinating ministry. These compassionate,
caring Christians are looking for solid teaching
and helpful guidance for spiritual healing. Dr. Day
has provided this and more.

He sets forth a wholistic understanding of healing, providing needed correction to approaches that
focus on only selected aspects of the healing process. Building from the healing ministry of Jesus,
Dr. Day defines health as a combination of harmo-

nious relationships, spiritual vitality, psychological maturity, and physical wellness. His frequently employed term "spiritual healing" does not refer to a narrow concept of healing apart from medicine, but rather an expanded understanding that all healing comes from God and that God uses many resources to achieve wholeness, health, and salvation. "Spiritual healing" is "one manifestation of the power and life and holiness of God. It is the result of the individual actively being open in every area of being to the reign of God. That result may be aided by those who have admitted God to the throne of their own lives and who, by reason of that fact, become the allies of God on the one hand and on the other hand the helpers of those who are trying to learn how to admit God and God's rule into their lives to heal sickness, purify the heart, illuminate the mind, and energize the will."

In the reprinting of this book, two changes have been made. The language has been broadened to be more inclusive of gender, and a study guide for reflection and discussion has been added.

A word about group sessions: The study guide for reflection and discussion is designed to promote personal sharing. The group leader should not rigidly follow the guidelines, but should instead be sensitive to the participants. Covenant with the group to pray for each other daily and to meet regularly, preferably once a week, to share reflections, questions, and insights. Doubts and disagreements are OK, too. Mutual support among like-minded companions can be serendipitous.

8

When you gather, come with a loving heart, an open mind, and a teachable spirit. Your shared time should be a special time to discover the mind and spirit of the healing Christ.

One more suggestion: Whether you are reading this book privately or in a group, saturate each study session with prayer and scripture. Take time at the beginning or end of each session to read one or two scripture passages that relate to healing (see Appendix One). Likewise, take time in each session for moments of intentional prayer. Allow the content and focus of your prayers to arise from the needs and emotions of the moment. Pray as the Spirit leads you.

A Prayer for the Guidance of the Holy Spirit

You may want to pray this prayer silently or as a group each time you come together.

> Come, Holy Spirit, enlighten my mind, cleanse my motives, clarify my intentions, and guide my ambitions, especially in this matter and mystery of healing.
>
> When full understanding is not possible,
> give me faith to trust in you anyway.
> When my questions are greater than my answers,
> give me faith to trust in you anyway.
> When my doubts outweigh my certainties,
> give me faith to trust in you anyway.

Above all else, Holy Spirit of the Living God, decrease my desire to live in my restrictive world of self and increase my desire to live in the freedom of your kingdom.

In the name of the One who makes possible the answers to this prayer, in the name of Jesus, I offer this request. Amen.

A special word of appreciation is extended to the following persons, who met to test the study guide. Their suggestions for improving the effectiveness of the guide have been incorporated into the final manuscript:

Charles and Erma Baird, Frances Williams, Frankie McConnell, Virginia Smith, Jo Walker, Leta Burnett, John Collett, Dee Hutchinson, Diana Smythe, Catherine Kirk, Mary Lou Wagner, Margie Smith, Kathleen Kunzelman, Rosalie Morris, Laura Flippen, Terrijean Crowell, Muriel Pilley, Lyvonne Gray, Betty Stroud, Cathy Turner, Kate Wells.

The editorial assistance of Marie Livingston Roy and Douglas Tonks is also acknowledged with sincere gratitude.

JAMES K. WAGNER
Nashville, Tennessee
1986

Introduction to the Original Edition

INCREASED INTEREST IN SPIRITUAL HEALING has been aroused among many preachers and laymen as a result of research and clinical activity in this field. To concerned Christians the term "spiritual healing" encompasses possibilities and potentialities for the wholeness of modern man's life—physical and mental, as well as spiritual.

No longer is the healing ministry of the Christian church looked upon as an illegitimate effort in "religious hocus-pocus." Students of the Christian faith agree as to the validity of spiritual healing, but they differ in their opinions as to the nature and extent of God's involvement in this area of human suffering.

Because of the increasing interest in the field of spiritual healing, Methodist Evangelistic Materials is privileged to present to Methodists the convictions of one Methodist minister, Dr. Albert Edward Day, who has given many years of leadership in the prayer and spiritual life movement within the Methodist church, and has been intimately involved in experiences of spiritual healing.

It is our hope that Methodists who read these *Letters* will approach them in the spirit of their author who says of others who have written about spiritual healing: "One may not agree with everything these authors have written, but in each one of them may be found much that will illumine the path that we must tread on our way to a solution of the problem that must be solved."

JOHN K. MCKEE, *Editor*
Methodist Evangelistic Materials
1964

Preface

MANY INTERESTING AND IMPORTANT EVENTS
are happening in the churches of our day—a new
and incisive self-criticism; a fresh concern for social relevance; a growing spirit of ecumenicity that
is holding out the hand of fellowship to those from
whom we have long been separated; theological
adventures in the direction of a more comprehen-
sive grasp of reality; biblical researches in behalf of
a better understanding of revelation; the application of psychological techniques to the cure of souls.

Not the least interesting is the new concern for
spiritual healing. The Episcopal church has its
Order of St. Luke, created to foster and guide the
practice of spiritual healing. The General Assem-
bly of the United Presbyterian Church raised a
commission of distinguished clergymen to study
the whole matter. That commission presented an
illuminating report which was adopted by the As-
sembly. Ministers here and there have quietly accepted the responsibility of a more direct ministry
to the sick, and with varied results have gone about
it in their own way. All who have undertaken it
have wished for more guidance in relation to the
many problems that arise. We all need to help each
other by sharing our experiences and insight.

It is with a desire to be helpful that these *Letters*
are published. They were written after twelve

years of humble but persistent effort to minister in the name of the healing Christ to the many who suffer and by their suffering are limited in their service to others. These *Letters* faithfully record the problems met, the solutions found, the heartbreaking failures as well as the gratifying successes encountered. They were addressed to a minister with a critical intelligence and with a passionate concern that his ministry to the people for whom Christ gave his life might be all that Christ intended it to be.

ALBERT EDWARD DAY
1964

My warm gratitude to Mrs. William Newitt, for her careful typing of this manuscript.

Letter 1
The Question of Involvement in Spiritual Healing

Dear Phillip,

It is good to hear from you once more. Your latest letter evokes new appreciation of your commitment to God and humanity. I have felt in you a spiritual potential not always present even in dedicated preachers, and I am not surprised by the big question you have now posed: "Should I undertake a healing ministry?"

You are just the kind of pastor to whom that question will come with real force. Your concern for people, your deep sorrow over the suffering which you encounter in your parish, your heartbreak over families broken by the untimely death of father or mother, your sadness over the loss of promising youth inevitably have made you wonder if there is something you might do to prevent such pain and bereavement.

I am keenly aware of your hesitation in assuming that what is usually called "spiritual healing" offers you the opportunity for an effective ministry to the afflicted. Your wide-ranging intelligence has acquainted you with the fanaticism that has attended many services of healing. You have been confronted with claims made by "healers" which were not substantiated by facts. You have also been distressed by the disillusionment of those who were promised healing but did not receive it. And when the call for help from the desperately ill and the impulse of your own caring heart have inspired you to pray with great earnestness for healing, no relief has apparently come.

So there you are, surrounded by people who love you and whom you love, wondering what more you can do for their bodies as well as their souls. The answer is not simple and easy. But there is an answer. Your dilemma also plagued me and compelled me in my own ministry to action. I do not pretend to have all the answers in any field, especially in this one. But in twelve years of serious, prayerful, continuous study and practice, some answers began to be evident.

If you want me to share them with you, I shall be glad to do so. It may require a number of letters between us—a kind of epistolary dialogue in which questions and answers, doubts and affirmations, stories of failures as well as successes are frankly and unhesitatingly recited. It will require the best thinking of which both of us are capable. But it can be an exciting adventure in which we may learn from each other, and through which we may emerge into a better understanding of the will of God for us and for our people, and a wider ministry to their bodies and minds and spirits.

I await your reply with great eagerness. In the meantime, may the grace of our Lord Jesus Christ be with you in both decision and duty.

A.E.

Letter 2
Contradiction and Paradox

Dear Phillip,

Your reply is further evidence of the genuine compassion and utterly sincere commitment which characterize your ministry to your people. So we shall begin our dialogue.

Your first question is just what a realistic mind and a truly pastoral heart would ask: "Is there any such thing as the healing of disease by spiritual means?" Unless the answer can be unequivocally affirmative, we are wasting our time in a discussion as futile as the old scholastic debate about how many angels can stand on the point of a needle. The real question should have been whether any angel ever did or could perform such an aerial feat or whether there are angels standing or sitting or flying anywhere. The basic question in our present dialogue is not how many persons have been spiritually healed of physical illness, but whether even one has had such a deliverance.

You cite a number of distressing instances of fraud or of illusion in this area. A woman, after being prayed for in the sight of thousands, threw away her crutches and walked off the platform, apparently miraculously cured; but she confessed afterward that she had received fifteen dollars for posing as a cripple on crutches. An old man, afflicted with deafness, was reportedly able to hear after his ears had been touched by the hands of a well-known healer; but when interviewed afterward, he was obviously still as deaf as ever.

A man, mentally ill with what a prominent writer on prayer diagnosed as demonic possession, was given the sacrament of exorcism and was pronounced cured by the exorcist; but soon afterward he took his own life.

You are baffled also by the fact that some practitioners in the field of spiritual healing have themselves died of cancer, and that others who have widely promoted the gospel of healing have watched their own beloved die in spite of many prayers offered by themselves and others.

I am glad that right at the beginning you have asked that we face such disturbing facts together. There are many like facts that will confront us as we pursue our dialogue. They account for much of the prevalent skepticism as to the possibility of spiritual healing. They delayed for a long time my own decision to undertake a healing ministry.

I had been much impressed by the large place the Gospel accounts give to the healing ministry of Jesus. I had associated with some dedicated people whose faith embraced the possibility of the healing of bodies as well as souls. I was sympathetic with their objectives, always fervently hoping that something would happen which would banish doubt and eliminate other possible explanations of apparent cures; nevertheless, doubts remained as to the validity of their assumptions and their conclusions.

When I brought some of my parishioners and my own beloved to the healing ministry of these modern-day apostles, there was no detectable therapeutic result. The deliverance from sickness, so movingly described as taking place hundreds of miles away, was not effected there before my eager eyes and hopeful heart. Once I had the opportunity to observe for a whole month at close hand the witness and the work of one who became nationally famous as preacher and healer. But what I saw left me in a quandary. Once or twice I recalled the plaint of the psalmist, "I said in my haste, all men [and some women] are liars" (Psalm 116:11, KJV).

Such a mood, however, was not long sustained. As I studied situations in which unhappy failures occurred, I became convinced that intentional fraud was rare. Most of the time it was evident that practitioners were under illusions about the factors present or the results achieved. Sometimes there had been wrong diagnosis. Sometimes the supposed cure of a named disease actually was only a momentary surge of emotion which for the time made the patients feel better, but actually left them no better as far as the real illness was concerned. The healer saw the temporary euphoria but not the sad aftermath. The reports of healing were sincere but mistaken. The healer carried away statistics, but left behind tragedy.

Sometimes the diagnosis was correct, but other factors besides the prayers of the healer were present. Treatments given by the doctor, medicines taken, the body's own amazing self-therapy, the patient's will-to-live—all had been at work and had reached their term; health was restored. In such instances it is not a simple matter to determine where the credit belongs. The haste to claim cures is unwise and often discredits the work of more humble and cautious ministers.

Physicians recognize the difficulties involved in making diagnoses, and that often diagnoses are in error. Cancer sometimes exists undetected and is cured by the body's own therapeutic activity. Neither the malignancy nor its mastery was discovered until some later operation for another condition revealed what had actually been the patient's history. Cancer is sometimes suspected when only ulcers are making trouble, if an ulcer merits the word "only." In all of these instances right prayer is relevant. The trust which it engenders fosters the body's own therapeutic activity. The fellowship with Christ, which is the heart of true prayer, challenges the condition that produces ulcers. The emotional purgation that comes through opening one's life to the God of love banishes the worry, the hate, the resentment, the anxiety, the jealousy which beget illness.

But what you and I are discussing is not the general relevance of prayer to all the coming and going of life. Prayer is important for the sick and the well, for the functions of the body and the operations of the mind, for those who have intolerable burdens to bear and for those whose lives appear free of adversity. We are agreed on that. Our question is, to put it bluntly, whether it is sensible to pray specifically for the healing of any or all diseases of the people of our parish as confidently as the doctor prescribes an antibiotic for some infection or sends a patient to the operating room for surgery. Is it ever possible to say that because we prayed this disease disappeared or that threatened death was prevented?

What makes this question even more poignant is the fact you have cited; namely, that ministers who have apparently prayed effectively for the healing of others have died of the very diseases for which they believed prayer to be the remedy; or, what is more distressing, have watched a spouse slip away while they and others have offered fervent supplications for the continuing presence of the spouse in the home so long blessed.

No one could be more conscious of the contradictions involved in such situations than I. You know of my own labors in this field and also of my own frustrations! While holding weekly services for healing in my own church and offering apparently effective prayers for the healing of sickness in my parish and elsewhere, I have seen the devoted mother of my children struggle against rheumatoid arthritis with great suffering and increasing helplessness. I have spent nights interceding for her healing. I have sought to share with her the faith I have cherished—that God's will is health for her and for all who will meet the conditions. I have brought to her those whom God had used elsewhere for the conquest of disease. But she still suffers and becomes more dependent upon others for the simplest necessities. I am not unaware of the challenge which her illness brings to the faith that has been, and still is, mine. One cannot write cheaply or speak lightly about the possibilities and realities of spiritual healing when one faces such a situation.

I will close for now and at the earliest possible moment return to this theme, which is engaging our people-centered concern.

A.E.

Letter 3
Evidence for the Reality of Spiritual Healing

Dear Phillip,

As you suggest, we will proceed at once to consider the problem with which my last letter closed; namely, the fact that so many prayers for healing, even in the most favorable cases, seem utterly to fail. Men and women who are long practiced in this ministry, when praying for persons whose integrity and faith would seem to make them ideal prospects for the operation of spiritual forces, often do encounter defeat.

One of my most heartbreaking experiences came when a beautiful young woman in my parish died of polio. She was a freshman in college, mentally alert, spiritually devoted—"the kind of person out of whom we hope to build America's tomorrow," as her anxious physician characterized her. She was a leader in our young adult group, a person with great charm, which she dedicated to the service of Christ. She hoped to become a Director of Christian Education. Swiftly came the blow. She was rushed to the hospital and put in an iron lung. A tracheotomy was performed to assure breathing.

Not only our prayer groups, but men and women of other faiths, Catholic and Jew, gave themselves to earnest prayer for her recovery. I spent hours upon hours by her side in intercession. But she went on to another life. Of that we had no doubt. Her body died but our faith and our love assured us that her spirit was in the keeping of him who is the resurrection and the life. But her family, her church, and this world where she is needed are bereft of her insight and inspiration.

She was not healed as Jesus healed people in Galilee and as we believe he can and does heal today. Why? We all grieved "not as others do who have no hope" (1 Thess. 4:13, RSV) but as those who had hoped that the healing Christ would deliver her from death for a life of service here. It was a sadness never to be forgotten and a mystery not then resolved.

Such experiences are numerous and very troubling. Unfortunately, they seldom get into discussions of spiritual healing. Healers tell vivid and moving stories of their successes. Their failures are buried in silence. That, you and I must not do. Any hypothesis that refuses to face its negations by reality is suspect and in the end a disaster. Any faith that cannot provide some interpretation for facts which challenge it is a very precarious faith and is likely to wither away under the pressures of circumstance.

What we need to recognize first of all is that we would never ask why some are not healed if we had not been persuaded that some are healed. If nobody is healed, then any particular instance of non-healing would not raise any question.

The second thing we need to keep in mind is that not even *materia medica* and surgery have universal success. "Can you take penicillin?" is the physician's question as he seeks to counteract an infection. He knows that for some people penicillin is not a remedy but an irritant. The personal equation is important in every illness and with every attempt to heal.

Why should we expect that spiritual therapy will be effective with every person for whom it is employed? The teaching and prayers of Jesus failed completely with Judas. The faith that healed multitudes healed only "a few sick folk" in Jesus' hometown.

A good physician will not abandon a practice because here and there remedies fail and a patient dies. But that physician will reexamine the treatments and seek to learn from failures. So, in my opinion, it is good sense not to let ourselves be dismayed by the failures that follow even our most devoted ministries. Rather should we reexamine ourselves and our techniques to discover why the failure has come.

The question you asked in the beginning is the right question. It is not, "Do prayers ever fail; is everybody healed by faith; is there no need of medicine or surgery?" The first and most basic question is this: "Is there any such thing as the healing of disease by spiritual means?" After that question has been answered, it will be time to inquire why failures come and what the conditions are that favor success.

The evidences for genuine spiritual healing are many and convincing.

First of all, there are the accounts in the four Gospels. Because of the reports of the investigations of expert historians into the New Testament records, some of our contemporaries have lost faith in the records themselves. It is assumed that so many myths and legends have accumulated around the Jesus of history that we are left without any authentic picture of what he was and did. Not only such stories as the feeding of the five thousand and the stilling of the storm on the Sea of Galilee and the raising of Lazarus, but also the reported healings which Jesus wrought are lightly dismissed as fiction by some.

The facts are, however, that many competent critics do not toss these healing wonders into the limbo of unhistorical accretions. Schubert Miles Ogden, in his *Christ without Myth*, declares that Rudolf Bultmann has not carried his own demythologization to its logical conclusion, and insists that the path must be trodden to its very end. Yet when Ogden states what he, himself, believes to be the "objective reality of the event Jesus Christ," he affirms "the entire reality of Jesus of Nazareth, including not only His preaching and *acts of healing* but His fellowship with sinners and His eventual death on the cross." Ogden says further that "the event of Jesus is but the representation in the form of a single human life of man's original possibility of existence," and that "in its deepest reaches it is nothing less than the God-man relationship that is the essentional reality of every human life."[1]

Gunther Bornkamm, whose *Jesus of Nazareth* has been hailed as an event in the intellectual history of our time, writes, "All those who turn to him in faith count on the power of Jesus which knows no bounds, and on the miracle which he can work, where all human help fails." Bornkamm adds that "there can be no doubt that the faith which Jesus demands, and which alone he recognizes as such, has to do with power and the miracle."[2]

With real confidence, therefore, we can read the Gospels and find in them not merely legends of healing, but healing itself.

What about our own time? Do actual healings also take place now? Perhaps the most impressive, especially for the skeptical mind, are the reports of the Medical Bureau at Lourdes, France. If you have not done so, I suggest that you get *The Miracle of Lourdes,* by Ruth Cranston. She was the daughter of Methodist Bishop Earl Cranston, and was herself a Methodist to the time of her death a few years ago. She visited Lourdes and spent months of research in its records and in personal visits to those who had been healed there. Her personal integrity vouches for the truthfulness of the report she made as a result.

What is perhaps the most convincing aspect of Miss Cranston's studies is the emphasis she laid upon the work of the Medical Bureau and her interpretation of its findings. The Bureau is not a Catholic institution. It is supported by physicians of all faiths, and no faith, from all over the world—scientists who are truly scientific in their desire to know what is happening at the famous shrine and to discover what those happenings mean for human welfare.

This is how the Bureau operates. Patients who come for treatment must bring with them certificates from the physicians who have diagnosed and treated them. If any of the pilgrims claim to have a cure, they must report to the Bureau at once for an examination. The results of that examination are entered into the records. But no matter how strong the evidence for a cure, the patient must return after a year for further examination before the Bureau will certify a cure.

The conditions for such certification are severe. The following questions must receive an affirmative answer from the participating doctors:

1. Did the illness described by the medical record exist at the moment of the patient's pilgrimage to Lourdes?
2. Was the malady suddenly stopped in its course at a time when there was no tendency toward improvement? Which symptoms disappeared at this time?
3. Is there a cure? Can you prove it with certainty? Did the cure take place without treatment?
4. Is it necessary to delay a decision?
5. (Finally, the ultimate question): Is there any possible medical explanation of this cure? In the present state of science, can any natural or scientific explanation be given?

"When the Medical Bureau at Lourdes is satisfied as to the genuineness of a cure, or if there is some question in their minds about it, the record of that cure—the documents, certificates, results of examinations, X-rays, bacteriological analyses, and everything to do with the case—is sent on to the Medical Commission. . . . The Commission makes a thorough study of the case, calling in such specialists as may be needed for more extensive observation. The duty of the Commission is not to declare a miracle, but is simply and solely to declare (or fail to declare) 'We find no natural or scientific explanation of this cure.'"[3] Surely any cure that passes such tests as these is authentic. Of these cures there are hundreds!

I was a member of a seminar composed of eminent physicians, surgeons, psychiatrists, physicists, clergy, and hospital chaplains who over a period of several years made a careful study of spiritual healing. The published reports of the seminar make arresting reading. The fifth report carried an introduction by Dr. Robert Laidlaw, at that time head psychiatrist of Roosevelt Hospital in New York City. In a remarkable statement, Dr. Laidlaw wrote, "To the question, 'does a healing power exist?' I believe we can answer with an unconditional 'yes.'"[4]

Physicians are rightly skeptical of healings reported here and there by ministers and laity. Physicians are the guardians of our health and would be lax in their responsibility if they did not eye with suspicion reports of cures effected by methods and under circumstances which do not commend themselves to critical judgment. I, myself, have often cringed at tall tales related by enthusiastic proponents of prayer therapy.

But in the light of sober accounts by reputable

practitioners across the country, as well as of these statements from Lourdes, I think we can answer in the affirmative the question you and I are considering; namely, is there any such thing as the healing of physical disease by spiritual means? If there were only one such instance, we would be justified in examining it, for it would represent the operation of a healing force in the realm of the spirit, which is our realm as ministers of Jesus Christ and about which we should be able to speak with authority.

I think I need now assure you that your reactions, positive or negative, will be most welcome. The important consideration is truth, and truth will most likely be ours if we are merciless with each other's opinions as well as confident of each other's integrity. "Where two or three are met together in my name, there am I in the midst." Christ is truth and this truth will be ours if our letters are a meeting in his name.

Letter 4
The Kingdom of God—Source of Healing Power

Dear Phillip,

It seems a long time since my last letter to you, and I have been eagerly awaiting your reply which arrived today.

Once more you have delighted me by your spontaneous contribution to our adventure—this time by the list of books you have been reading in search of a sound foundation for our mutual discussion. Leslie D. Weatherhead's *Psychology, Religion, and Healing;* George G. Dawson's *Healing: Pagan and Christian*; Flanders Dunbar's *Mind and Body*; Karl Heim's *The Transformation of the Scientific World View* are solid foundations on which one may build an individual structure of thought. One may not agree with everything these authors have written, but in each one of them may be found much that will illumine the path that we must tread on our way to a solution of the problems that must be solved.

In addition, I suggest some other books which will provide clinical material for our examination: *The Healing Power of Faith*, by William Charles Oursler; *A Reporter Finds God Through Spiritual Healing*, by Emily Gardiner Neal; *Fulfilling*, by Dorothy Kerin; *I Believe in Miracles* by Kathryn Kuhlmann; *The Ministry of Healing*, by John E. Large; *The Case for Spiritual Healing*, by Donald Gross.

In my last letter I reported to you the sources of that evidence which to me is convincing proof that the spiritual healing of physical as well as mental illness is a reality.

The question we must now consider is how to account for such healings. What is the healing force at work in them?

Some of the factors in any healing process are readily identifiable: the life-force within the body itself; the will-to-live of the patient; the meaningfulness the patient has found in life which gives an urgency to go on living; faith in God and in the physician; the sense of being loved and needed; the medicines prescribed; and the physiotherapy employed. All of these play an important role in recovery, and their function in this respect is recognized.

But in specifically spiritual healing, as we designate it, another factor is present. IT IS GOD. "The Lord is the healer," is the way one writer has identified it. The New Testament says it another way, "If it is by the finger of God that I am expelling evil spirits, then the kingdom of God has swept over you unawares" (Luke 11:20, PHILLIPS). And, again, Jesus referred to the healings that attended His ministry as "the demonstrations of God's power" (Matt. 11:21, PHILLIPS).

From the beginning to the end of Jesus' ministry, the emphasis is upon the kingdom of God as the source from which come life and healing power. To "seek first the kingdom of God" is to find everything that makes life worthwhile—"all these things shall be added to you." Over and over again in parables Jesus is inviting people into this kingdom, is telling them the secret of entrance into the kingdom. Over and over again in his ministry he reveals the amazing things that happen to people as "the kingdom of God comes nigh to you."

The discovery of the meaning of the kingdom of God for the individual and for society has been one of the most thrilling experiences of my life. It has given me a concept of spiritual healing that makes it a gospel both in its joyous promise and in its rational demands. The gospel of spiritual healing is not an offer of "cheap grace"; it is an offer of grace sufficient for every human life. It offers not immunity from life, but ability for life. It is not an excuse for ignorance of nature's laws or defiance of those laws, but rather an insight into the role of laws and a mastery of laws for the sake of results not possible if nature is left to itself. It offers an ever present possibility of victory, not only over temptation but also over disease. It is the gift of health and sanctity.

I want to be very explicit at this point, especially because of the contemporary mood in theology. Paul Tillich and Dietrich Bonhoeffer and Bishop J. A. T. Robinson have stirred up some hornets' nests among theologians as well as laity. But they have also spoken to something in the minds and hearts of people who are very serious about religion, but who have found great difficulty in that orthodoxy which seems to make God a super-being in the sky who invades our human world on errands of mercy or judgment.

There can be no doubt that our contemporary world is, as Samuel Howard Miller describes it, "scrubbed clean of special events divinely arranged, deprived of . . . the outright arrogance of miracle." It also seems true that the faith of modern people is likely to be in "a God whose acts are not separable from existence itself; a God in whom we must have faith, not because we have been overwhelmed by direct epiphanies, but because God's glory pervades the common structure of things."[5]

So the debate rages on, between those who believe in a personal God and those who have a structural God; between those who want us "to teach the simple lesson that we all were created by a personal God to whom we will ultimately be accountable," and those "who are hungry for a faith concerning the meaning of life and yet who cannot stomach the words and phrases we use when we try to express the gospel"; between those who say, "I am seeing so-and-so and I must put an hour aside first to pray for this person," and those who say, "I am really praying for people . . . precisely as I meet them and really give my soul to them"; between those who believe "in waiting upon the Lord" and those who insist upon high-powered "holy hustle."

As I have read these debaters, it seems to me that they are saying both too much and too little. Some are expecting from God what they must do for themselves; others are demanding of themselves what only God can do. They leap out of the frying pan of sizzling supernaturalism into the fire of an inadequate humanism. They try to get God down

34

from the sky, and then they lose God in the mechanisms of nature and the contingencies of humanity.

They are so afraid of anything that smacks of "miracle" that they reduce us and God to the formulas of the laboratory and the frolics of the subconscious. If they honor the Divine as Creator, they discharge God from the role of Sustainer and are in great confusion as to God's function as Redeemer. In all their aversion to making God an object among other objects, they come very near to making God a subject indistinguishable from all other subjects, especially themselves.

I hope we may not get bogged down in the mire of such confusion. For that reason I suggest that we look at the thrilling idea of the kingdom of God as Jesus envisaged it and lived by it.

To put it in the simplest terms, the kingdom of God is the reign of God. Wherever God reigns, whether in the life of an individual or in any segment or institution of society, there is the kingdom of God. The nature of God is revealed in the lives and situations where the Divine reigns. God is always near to every life, seeking admission and permission to rule: "Behold I stand at the door and knock." Therefore, the kingdom is near to every life; the power and vitality and sanctity of that kingdom are near to every life.

Spiritual healing is one manifestation of the power and life and holiness of God. It is the result of the individual actively being open in every area of being to the reign of God. That result may be aided by those who have admitted God to the throne of their own lives and who, by reason of that fact, become the allies of God on the one hand and on the other hand the helpers of those who are trying to learn how to admit God to rule in their lives to heal sickness, purify the heart, illuminate the mind, and energize the will.

That brief synopsis is the essence of the substance of my own faith in spiritual healing. Keep it in mind as we proceed with our correspondence. As long as we are two and not echoes of each other, there is promise that our journey will lead to fresh discoveries and greater understandings. We need each other's antithesis if our final synthesis is to make any real contribution to our work as ministers of Jesus Christ.

A.E.

Letter 5
The God of the Kingdom

Dear Phillip,

You say rightly that I began with the kingdom of God but did not identify the God of the kingdom, nor define the manner of God's reign, nor clearly relate God and the kingdom to our sicknesses and sins.

Where do I locate God? When I have, how do I conceive God? What is the manner of God's action upon us? How do we assure ourselves of the divine action we need? What are the conditions of receiving God's power for health? Those are your questions.

I do not locate God! That would truly make God an object. The one thing I must say is to affirm God's all-relatedness. If you think in terms of space, it seems necessary to affirm God's everywhereness. If you think in terms of action, one must affirm God's immediacy. If you think in terms of concern for you, "the very hairs of your head are numbered."

If you ask how I conceive God's relationship with us, it is as the living, loving, personal, continuing Source of our life. "In God we live and move and have our being." To talk about a God *up there* or *down here* or *underneath* or *round about* or *within* is to impose our human geography and geometry upon a heavenly being. I want to get away from that

37

to reality—to a reality that makes God the source of the authentic reality of me.

There is much in me that is not authentic—much that was superimposed by parental training, by social influences, by the accidents of existence; much that my own egocentricity and pride and fear have twisted into a caricature of my real self; much that is the result of what I have done to myself and what others have done to me. The tragedy in this is that what I have derived from my living source in God is marred sometimes almost beyond recognition.

But here is the blessed fact, the most blessed of all facts: the God who is the source of my authentic self which has become inauthentic—a mockery of the divine intention—is still right here. Still God offers to be the source of new and better life, diviner thoughts, holier emotions, and nobler actions.

Just as in Jesus God ate and drank with the publicans and sinners, God eats and drinks with me.

Just as in Jesus God said to the woman in the dust, "Neither do I condemn thee; go, and sin no more," so God is constantly saying to me, "Do not lie there in the dust of self-contempt; arise and go out with me to a new life of moral victory and self-giving service."

Just as in Jesus God prayed, "forgive them for they know not what they do," so God looks in upon my folly and mediates the forgiveness I need and must have if I am to rise to walk in newness of life.

Just as again and again in Jesus God asked persons to deny themselves, take up their cross and follow the way, so is God ceaselessly urging me to deny my egocentric self, take up the cross of loyalty and love, and follow the way to one Calvary after another.

My dear friend, I am terribly conscious of my failures and my inadequacies and my ignorance and my too human reaction to life. But I am also thrillingly conscious that the God of Jesus Christ is a source from which ceaselessly come aspiration and inspiration to be more like Christ and God, thoughts too deep for tears, impulses too high for my low moods but not too high for that which I may become if I will let God lift me to new planes of life. From God come love for the unlovable, dreams for the dreamless, and patience for the unendurable.

And as all this is happening to me and within me, I know it is not just "me." Yet I know also that it is what I am meant to be. This God is not "me," and yet is not alien to me. I am not God, and yet I do respond to God. In my best moments I feel at home with God. In my worst moments I do not feel at home even with myself.

I know that God is God and not human; yet I also know that God created humanity in the divine image. I know that humanity in its blindness often shuts itself away from God; yet I also know that God can never be shut away from humanity. God is the everlasting source from which I receive whatever of real life is mine and from whom I may receive eternal life here and now, if I will but open the gates of self to God's abundance.

God will make my heart, my mind, my body into the kingdom if I will allow it. God will not reign, God cannot reign, without my consent; yes, without my cooperation. Given that consent and cooperation, new and otherwise impossible events begin to happen—illumination, conquest over temptation, healing for the body.

I am more and more confident that what so often defeats our ministry is our poverty of expectation. Our poverty of expectation is that we assume that everything depends on us. Our witness is of what we have done for God, and not what God has done for us. We think and act as if it is our kingdom that we are having to build for God's sake, and not God's kingdom in which God is ruling and acting for our sake; that it is our reputation that is at stake, not God's; that it is our credit and not God's glory that accrues whenever the good and the true and the beautiful appear on the scene.

We often talk about healing as if nothing beyond the calculable effects of medicine, surgery, or psychiatry appear. "We bind the wound, God heals it"—that is a more accurate description. God is at work wherever medicine and surgery and deep analysis work a cure. God is in the laboratory and the operating room and by the analyst's couch. The chemist, the physician, the surgeon, the psychiatrist are working with God if they are working effectively for the sake of health.

We must not think of God as a personal energy off alone and humanity at work in healing off by itself. If we do that, we are guilty of the "God-in-the-sky, people-on-earth" fallacy. It is not true that human-ity is self-existent and God self-isolated until by some religious act God is brought into the picture to correct and reinforce. People breathe and feel and think and act only because God is enabling them. Whenever the mind of someone is quickened to nobler conceptions of duty, whenever the heart of someone is stirred to compassion, whenever the will of someone is nerved to heroic deed, God is on the scene—the source of all that is true and kind and brave.

God is distinct from humanity but is not distant from humanity. None of us would live for a moment if God were to withdraw from us or if we could absolutely separate ourselves from God. Forget the semantic antics of those who insist that God must be up or down, outside or inside, in the heights or in the depths. God is where God acts. *God is here* wherever we are—here as the Source of our life; here as the Creator and Sustainer of what we are; here as the Challenger of what we have done to God's creation in us; here as Forgiver of our sins against God; here as Re-creator of the marred im-age we have become; here as Healer of our diseases of body, mind, and soul. Whatever is normal in us is that which God sustains. Whatever is abnormal or subnormal is that which God is here to help us correct.

Whenever we talk about spiritual healing, we are therefore not suggesting that some miracle is necessary to bring God on the scene, or that some natural laws are violated by the insurgence of divine pity into a situation from which God has until that moment been absent. We are only, but imperfectly, saying that the God always present, but limited by humanity's ignorance or unbelief or self-will, has been given a free hand in humanity's life. We are saying that God has been invited to reign in a life where self has been on the throne; that God's kingdom has become more truly a reality in that life; that that person has entered the kingdom of God.

The kingdom of God has a tremendous social significance. But its impact upon society awaits its realization in the lives of individuals. "Thy kingdom come, *beginning with me*." It must begin here, or it cannot operate in the social order. Its agents are not "principalities and powers" operating from the unseen; but persons operating on the scene, infusing a new spirit, creating new institutions, writing new laws, inaugurating a new era. It came near in Jesus—"the kingdom of God has come upon you" (Luke 11:20, RSV). It has been coming ever since where men and women first enthrone God in their own lives.

It is on such an enthronement that real spiritual healing depends. After I hear from you, I want us together to look at the authentic word of Jesus as he speaks about the impact of the reign of God upon our plodding lives.

A.E.

Letter 6
Jesus' Concept of the Kingdom—
Charter for Spiritual Healing

Dear Phillip,

I feel that the time is ripe for us together to look at the utterances of Jesus about the kingdom of God. Because you are a persistent student of the Gospels and are informed by patient reading of the conclusions of sound historical scholarship, as well as by your own devotional study of the records, I need only indicate the places where Jesus spoke so arrestingly about the possibilities of human life in which God is enthroned.

As we have said in our earlier letters, the kingdom of God means the reign of God. It means God having the right of way in one's life, in one's thinking, choosing, acting. It means accepting God's stance, adopting God's attitudes, sustaining the relationships which God would approve as far as all these are made known to us and fostered in us by God's spirit.

It means what is implied in the exhortation, "Let go and let God." But it also means, "Take hold in God's name, and hold fast." It means "Have thine own way, Lord," but also, "My body, soul, and spirit, Jesus, I give to thee." It means, "Thy will be done," but also "I will to do thy will." It means relying on the grace of God, but it also means summoning one's own grit for the sustained effort involved in unseating the egocentric self and enthroning God.

It means not only "accepting Christ" but "taking up one's cross and following him." The kingdom of God involves what God can and will do in our lives, and also what we must do for a life in God.

Since the central interest in our letters just now is the often misunderstood matter of true spiritual healing, let us briefly survey the meaning of the kingdom of God as it relates to our topic. To me the relationship is very convincing and enlightening and, if I may use that much abused word, thrilling.

It is obvious that, in the mind of Jesus, to be in the kingdom is to be on the way to true greatness. One of the most startling things Jesus ever said was his comment on John the Baptist. He had a high opinion of John: "Never has there appeared on earth a mother's son greater than John the Baptist" (Matt. 11:11, NEB). That was a tribute to make the student of history stop and ponder. But Jesus quickly added, "Yet the least in the kingdom of Heaven is greater than he."

If the first statement halts one, the second overwhelms one. Jesus evidently believed with all his heart that the kingdom of heaven brings with it more than all the cultures and societies in history; that to be in the kingdom is to be endowed with such greatness as no morality and no religious system can impart; that the kingdom is not merely a set of rules to be obeyed, but an offer to be accepted, a benefaction to be received, a kind of holy ordination for great service to God and humanity.

So he taught men to pray "Thy kingdom come"; to "seek first the kingdom of God and his right-

44

eousness"; to "enter the kingdom"; to "receive the kingdom of God as a little child"; to regard the kingdom as a pearl of such value that one will sell all that one has and purchase it; to cut off a hand or pluck out an eye if they jeopardize one's entrance into the kingdom; to proclaim the kingdom as the ultimate meaning of life.

His greatest disciple, Paul, summarized the nature of the kingdom and its offer to people as "Things beyond our seeing, things beyond our hearing, things beyond our imagining, all prepared by God for those who love him" (1 Cor. 2:9, NEB).

After meditating upon the range of Jesus' teaching about the kingdom and Paul's witness to what living in and for the kingdom meant to him, one begins to wonder why we have ever turned away from the kingdom to little dukedoms of our own. One wonders also why our preaching is often so thin and our living is so poverty-stricken and so devoid of grandeur. There is so much to offer humankind in the name of the kingdom, and we offer so little.

A critical study of the New Testament leaves little room for doubt that one of the great benedictions of the kingdom is its gift of health. That is explicit again and again in the teaching of Jesus.

Recall the time when John sent his messengers to Jesus. John had preached that the kingdom of heaven was at hand. He had high hopes that Jesus was to inaugurate such a kingdom. But John himself was in prison and found his lot hard to reconcile with the promise of the kingdom. Would the kingdom of God permit its herald to languish in jail? So he sent his messengers to Jesus with a straight challenge, "Are you really what I believed you to be, or is all this just another hoax?" The reply of Jesus was significant. He did not argue with the messengers or try to make out a case for himself and his mission. He simply told them to go and tell John what they had seen, how "the blind recover their sight, the lame walk, the lepers are clean, the deaf hear, the dead are raised to life, the poor are hearing the good news" (Matt. 11:5, NEB).

It all seemed to say to John: "This is the kingdom which you and I both believed to be near. It is not a kingdom of this world such as you expected. Its power is not political or military. Its objective is not control over lives but the healing of diseases, the forgiveness of sins, the conquest of human hearts, the illumination of minds, the creation of a fellowship of love. This is already being achieved. Blessed is the person who does not lose faith in me and in the kingdom!"

Recall, too, another illustration of the nature of the kingdom. Jesus is pictured as sending out twelve disciples on a mission. He tells them to "heal the sick, raise the dead, cleanse lepers." And he enjoins them to say as they do all this, "The kingdom of Heaven is upon you" (Matt. 10:7, 8, NEB).

Again, Jesus was challenged by his opponents who said that he cast out devils "by Beelzebub the prince of devils." Jesus quickly showed them the fallacy of their assumption and added, "But if it is by the finger of God that I drive out the devils, then be sure the kingdom of God has already come upon you" (Luke 11:20, NEB).

However, it is not in such incidents as these that the relationship between the kingdom of God and the healing of disease is most convincingly demonstrated. Rather, it is in two simple but decisive facts.

First, there can be no doubt that the chief emphasis of Jesus and his supreme devotion was the kingdom of God. Second, neither is there any real doubt that an authentic history of Jesus of Nazareth reveals the very large role the healing of sickness played in his ministry. What can those two facts mean, if not that health is a concern of the kingdom of God and that the God of the kingdom can and does act in behalf of health and wholeness?

Here, it seems to me, is our charter for a ministry to the sick and a clue to the way that ministry can best find its fulfillment. The kingdom of God must be the object of our overmastering dedication and our chief reliance. If the kingdom of God means what Jesus said it does, then we are not only authorized to dedicate ourselves to the healing of sickness but also to count upon the help of God in such an undertaking.

If we accept such a charter and come to an intelligent comprehension of its meaning, we shall be saved from the fanaticism that often corrodes the adventure of spiritual healing. We also shall begin to find answers to such questions as the following: What are the conditions of healing? Why are some people healed and not others?

47

Now, we have come to the most delicate and yet the most important part of our correspondence. There is much mystery about matters that we shall consider. As long as I have worked in this field, I am still making and trying out hypotheses. About some issues I am still in a quandary. About some others I feel that the venture of faith is still called for. Let us join in prayer that the spirit of truth may guide us.

A.E.

Letter 7
Membership in the Kingdom—
the Condition of Healing

Dear Phillip,

We are venturing into areas where there are few reliable maps and where many sincere people have lost their way. We are aware of the prevalent misadventures in this field. We have been disturbed by uncritical and often arrogant assumptions that have made the very term "spiritual healing" seem to be the synonym of nonsense. We have seen the blind lead the blind until both fell into the ditch. Our caution is perhaps our best equipment of our undertaking.

But we must not permit caution to veto the necessary risks which are involved in the quest for truth. We are mountain climbers seeking to reach a difficult summit. One of the rules in such ascents is to keep looking up and not down, especially where there is a yawning abyss below. There are abysses which have claimed some fellow explorers. If this is not to be our fate, we must not let the abysses hypnotize us. Let us hopefully and prayerfully keep looking up. We shall never be rash, I hope. But we must be bold and not fear to move where logic and faith direct us.

Having located the charter for spiritual healing in Jesus' teaching and practice of the kingdom of God, it seems obvious that from here on we must be guided by the laws and spirit of the kingdom.

That means, first of all, that the conditions of healing are those which determine our entrance into the kingdom and its entrance into us, our continuance in it, and our receptivity to its blessings.

Some people become very nervous and even hostile when anyone talks about conditions of healing. Their insistance on the divine initiative makes any inquiry into our human response seem superfluous. Their interpretatin of God's grace leads them to assume that God acts not only without any consideration of our merit, but even without any demand for possible changes in our attitudes or our way of life. It is true that the initiative is with God.

> I sought the Lord, and afterward I knew
> He moved my soul to seek Him, seeking me;
> It was not I that found, O Savior true;
> No, I was found of thee.[6]

That is always true of any legitimate search for God, whether for forgiveness, or light, or comfort, or help in the battle with evil—or healing! God is more eager to get at us than we are to find God and God's life. The psalmist did not exaggerate when he wrote, "Thou art he who took me from the womb." It is God who is always trying to take us from where we are to where we ought to be in God's love.

> Like tides on a crescent sea-beach,
> When the moon is new and thin,
> Into our hearts high yearnings

50

Come welling and surging in—
Come from the mystic ocean,
Whose rim no foot has trod,—
Some of us call it longing,
And others call it God.[7]

Inspiration precedes aspiration. God always in-
spires the quest for what only God can be and give
and do!

It is also true that none of us ever can merit God's
gifts and action and comradeship. People often say,
"I am not good enough to expect God to heal me."
The answer is, "Of course you are not good enough.
No one is. If healing of body or mind or spirit depended upon an adequate goodness on our part,
there would be no healing of anybody anywhere."

But while the initiative is always with God, response and cooperation are always required of people. "Work out the salvation that God has given you
with a proper sense of awe and responsibility. For it
is God who is at work within you, giving you the
will and the power to achieve his purpose" (Phil.
2:12, 13, PHILLIPS).

As true as it is that we can never earn God's gifts,
it is also true that conditions are always attached to
God's giving. If we want forgiveness, we must forgive (Matt. 6:14,15). If we want light, we must open
our eyes (Matt. 6:22). If we want comfort, we must
come to Christ (Matt. 11:28). If we want help we
must renounce our self-sufficiency (Matt. 5:3).

What then is the cooperation, *what are the conditions required for spiritual healing?* Since healing

follows the right relationship with the kingdom of God, the answer lies in the nature of the kingdom itself and upon our response to the character and will of God.

To say it in another way, God acts in healing where God reigns. God does not reign where God's will is flouted. Then God must act with vigor, but as an opponent. "The face of the Lord is against them that do evil." God acts in defense of the kingdom. God acts to save people, if possible, from themselves. God acts to save others from the evils of the evil doer, if that be possible. Such actions are judgment. They are not actions in anger, actions in revenge, or actions to destroy; but actions to bring people to their senses, to make them aware of their folly, and to effect such changes in people as will change their ways and open the way for God into their lives.

Only where God truly reigns, where God's will is accepted, where the obedience and cooperation of people give God a free hand in their lives can God give them health in the place of disease, truth in the place of error, holiness in the place of vileness, and beauty for ashes.

The prime condition for healing is therefore to enter the kingdom, to let God reign, to give God a free hand in one's life. This is quite a different thing from accumulating merit, earning God's blessing, establishing a goodness which can be offered as the purchase price of healing; and it is not saying that only the perfect can be healed. This is something much more rational and much more within the reach of us all. We cannot make ourselves worthy of

God; we can give ourselves to God. We cannot eradicate all that is ungodlike within, but we can abdicate in God's favor and let God undertake the job.

Such a giving of ourselves is a much more serious thing than we sometimes make it. It is often parodied, and the actors in the parody afterward wonder why nothing significant has happened to them—why they are not forgiven and healed and renewed. They have not really given themselves over to God; they have merely made a declaration of intention; they have for a little while indulged in a propitious mood; they have announced an engagement. But they have not followed the declaration with a signing of the deed; they have not made the mood of the moment a real surrender; the engagement did not result in a marriage. There has been no real change in themselves. Self is still on the throne while God is permitted only an advisory function, with advice most of the time unheeded.

Really letting God reign is serious business. It is not merely a folding of the hands in nonresistance. It is taking our rebellious, resisting, squalling self with both hands and laying it on the altar.

It is not merely singing "Have Thine Own Way, Lord"; it is halting our own impulsive way and waiting for God to point out the way.

It is not merely conforming our habits and attitudes to those who belong to our class and our church; it is a readiness to break with our class and our church, if necessary, in order to learn from God the attitudes and practices which belong to the kingdom.

It is not merely giving God the privilege of brush-

53

ing the dust off our habitual mode of life; it is actually a dying with Christ that we might rise to walk in newness of life.

It is more than having "the old person" dressed in a new suit by the generosity of God. It is giving permission for "the old person" to be sentenced to death that "the new person in Christ" may begin to be.

Recognition of all this will save spiritual healing from being confused with the magic which presumes to entangle God in the cure of the ailments of men and women who have no intention of serving God but want only to be relieved of their pains and guaranteed the health that will let them live longer to serve the devil. It will deliver the church from those ministers who see in healing only another gadget with which to interest the unrepenting crowd and fill church treasuries with tainted money. It will provide answers to those sincere people who need from God that which their physicians and surgeons have not been able to provide and who, believing that God can heal, want to know what they must do to make God's healing possible.

To summarize it all: God can and does heal where God is permitted to reign. Our responsibility is to offer the throne in our lives to God.

A.E.

Letter 8
Nature of Membership in the Kingdom

Dear Phillip,

You are right in saying that "enthroning God in our lives" is a sadly misunderstood affair. The instances you have cited illustrate how easy it is to assume that God is on the throne, when in fact God is actually still knocking at the door.

It has been my lot to encounter a number of persons of whom this is true. Their commitment has been noisy but woefully incomplete. They have claimed to be crucified with Christ, when they have not even watched his crucifixion from a confusing distance. They say their "all is on the altar," when actually most of it is carefully under lock and key to keep God or anyone else from getting at it. They affirm that they do what they do under orders from God, when most orders from God are sidetracked for the impulses of their ego. They quote scripture, but it is scripture twisted to support outworn tradition and impregnable prejudice.

In all such instances the reign of God is a misnomer for the reign of self, the reign of tradition, the reign of custom, the reign of religiosity, the reign of sentiment, the reign of perverted mysticism.

God does the best that can be done for such people, but that best is but a fraction of what might be done if God were given a free hand. God's patient, ever-seeking, ever-compassionate love often breaks through into their routines to give a glimmer of new light, to avert a disaster threatened by their rebelliousness, to touch their dust and awaken it to a dream of greatness. So even they can say that God has helped them, that they have been conscious of God's help, that unexpected and undeserved good has come their way.

But because God does not actually reign in their minds and hearts, the day-by-day victories which life needs are not theirs; the healing for which they pray does not take place; the "pageant of triumph" of which Paul wrote is replaced by a tattered parody—mournful to behold and heartbreaking to be a part of.

What then does it mean to have God actually reign in a human life? Simply, to have the will of God as the final authority. Or, more accurately, *to will to have God's will the final authority.* This is not striving for an absurd moral perfectionism. It is an earnest, genuine, ceaselessly renewed moral intention. It points the whole life toward the discovery of God's will and relies on the grace of God to help obey that will. It is the reverse of impulsive living. It is the refusal of repetitive conduct. It is the rejection of custom and tradition as arbiters in the daily round. It is a truly divine discontent with commonly accepted behaviors and socially praised achievements. It is an every-morning-awaiting-new-light-from-heaven on the day's tasks. It is a continuing query, "What wilt thou have me to do?"

To will the will of God in one's life does not mean strain and stress and fret and anxiety, all of which are self-defeating. It does not mean grim and glum and gritty enslavement to the minutiae of life. One does not attempt to enthrone God in life unless one trusts God's wisdom and love and power. Such trust, therefore, makes the quest for the discovery of God's will a joyful quest of love. It quickens the mind and enthralls the heart. It keeps one open and expectant and confident. That in turn makes more likely the finding of the ultimate will. It turns life into a romance. It has its rigors, as all deep romance does; but they are the rigors of the alert mind and the bounding heart and the patient will.

Even so, however, the reign of God will never be complete in any life. It is still a human life, not the reproduction of the life of God. It will still have its unconquered territory, its undiscovered hinterlands, its precarious hold on reality. But it will be ever becoming more and more God's kingdom and, therefore, the scene of the wondrous works of God in body, mind, and spirit. It will be the life in which one will more likely experience revelation, sanctity, wholeness, and what we call healing.

Such a life will not forget that the quest for the will of God does not begin with one's own effort. There have always been some people who have earnestly sought the reign of God for their own lives and for the life of society. Nor have they sought in vain. God has not left humanity without a witness anywhere, in any age.

Our quest today is historically conditioned. Each one of us in a large measure is the creation of all the yesterdays of humankind. The impact of yesterday is registered in laws and customs and institutions which largely influence our thinking. Creed and code, which are imperfect, nevertheless have something to say to all people who seek to know the will of God for their lives. To neglect them is to make our quest more difficult and more liable to error.

When the rich young ruler came to Jesus asking, "What shall I do to inherit eternal life?" Jesus quickly pointed him to the Ten Commandments. And in Jesus' parable of the rich man and Lazarus, the rich man, unable to escape the hell of his own selfishness, begs that Lazarus be sent to warn his five brothers lest they come to the same sad end. But he is told, "They have Moses and the prophets: they can listen to them. . . . If they will not listen to Moses and the Prophets, they would not be convinced even if somebody were to rise from the dead" (Luke 16:29, 31, PHILLIPS).

History has much to say to us that will unveil the will of God. It is never as if we had to start from scratch. Nor is it good sense to assume that the real quest begins with our own pilgrimage toward the kingdom. If that were our situation, we might well despair.

On the other hand, if God is to reign in our lives, we cannot be the slaves of history. "New occasions teach new duties." Jesus said over and over again, "You have heard it said . . . but I say unto you." He did not hesitate to break with tradition. He was God's pioneer, for only thus could the kingdom of God come to him and, through him, to his time and to our contemporary need. In a real sense every one who seeks the kingdom must be a pioneer.

The reign of God is a continuity from age to age, but it is also a revolution in every age. If we simply go on imitating our ancestors, we shall find ourselves at war with the kingdom again and again. It is even true that we cannot imitate our own yesterdays if we are to do the will of God today. The saints have always known that. The rest of us, who are not saints, must learn this truth from them.

"Tenting on the old camp ground" may awaken tender memories but it will not keep us in creative touch with God. For all who would have their lives to be the scene of "operation-kingdom-of-God," it must be that they nightly pitch their "moving tent a day's march nearer home."[8]

The reign of God is not the static affair many have easily assumed it to be. Those who make it so malign God and maltreat their own lives. Nor is it the half-hearted acceptance of formal rules. It is the realm of a creative God who said, "Behold, I make all things new"; who is the master of detail; and who, without fussiness but with love's tender concern for our fulfillment, summons us to live in day-by-day response to the growing revelation of God.

All of this is intimately related to the gospel of healing and is essential to the wise proclamation of it.

A.E.

59

Letter 9
Health and Wholeness God's Will for All

Dear Phillip,

Your latest letter poses what is undoubtedly the most perplexing question in regard to the history and practice of spiritual healing: *Why are the healings comparatively few in comparison with the many who are not healed?* If ever you and I need to be absolutely frank with each other, it is as we face this question.

It was at this point that I suffered many a disillusionment in my contacts with practitioners and advocates of spiritual healing. Not only did I witness many failures in their work, but I was distressed that they refused to admit failure. People for whom they prayed died prematurely or from prolonged agonizing disease as their sufferings continued unabated. Instead of recognizing what had actually happened, some would say: "We did pray for the healing of sickness, and our prayer was answered. God has taken the sufferer to the land-of-no-more-pain. He will never be sick again. He is healed permanently." Or if failure was admitted, all responsibility for failure was laid upon the person for whom prayer was offered; either there was lack of faith, hidden sin, or inner rebellion of some sort.

No doubt either of these conditions would make any healing difficult, as we shall see later. But my own observations at the time seemed to indicate a rationalization of failure instead of a true account of the whole situation.

Later, when with some timidity but with a real sense of urgency I began seriously and systematically to offer prayer for healing, I encountered this problem head-on. People were healed who seemed most unlikely prospects for such a divine favor. Others were not healed whose quality of life seemed to guarantee that, if God ever healed anybody, it would be they.

In an earlier letter I told you of that brilliant and beloved college freshman who was smitten with polio and for whom I and many others prayed, but who died after an illness of a few days. Recently I had a similar experience with the beautiful mother of two children, the beloved wife of a gracious friend and a cultural leader in the community. She wanted so much to live and had everything to live for. She was responsive to our teaching and cooperative with all that we tried to do for her. The hours spent at her side in prayer and conversation about God and God's love are a precious memory. Her death had none of the bitterness of defeat but was a witness to faith's triumph over death. But she did die and left bereaved hearts and an impoverished world behind her. In other cases life continued but with great suffering and serious limitation of activity, if not complete helplessness.

On the other hand, there were healings where there was the least real expectation on our part and, seemingly, the absence of the faith and dedication which we thought an essential condition for the operation of healing grace.

A young man was smitten with a brain condition for which only an operation offered hope of relief. But the operation was so dangerous that its promise of relief was shadowed by its threat of death. The operation was set for the next morning. Prayers were offered that the surgeon would delay the operation and give God a chance to heal. When the surgeon came the next morning he was aware that something had happened. The operation was postponed. It never took place. In a few days the man was home and well and has never had a return of the affliction.

That, too, is not a rare experience. For reasons which we are going to explore together, men and women whose piety was not impressive and about whom it was difficult to marshal any vivid expectation were healed of their sickness and went on to normal but not impressively pious lives. It was very baffling.

Often there are remissions in even malignant diseases when the patient recovers without the intervention of medicine or surgery. The physician can give no account of such recoveries except to credit nature's own therapeutic action. And so it would not be amiss to assume that some of these cures to which I have just referred were not the result of prayer but had occurred because the life-force within had succeeded in defeating death.

That of course does not mean that God had nothing to do with it, for we ought to recognize this life-force as God at work. But that still leaves our question unanswered. Why does this life-force, which is God at work, manifest itself in the bodies of persons

63

who are apparently least concerned with and least open to God? And why does it not prevail in the illnesses of persons who are most devoted to God and most sensitive to find and do God's will?

In every other therapy both success and failure follow the prescribed treatment. We do not discount the success or deny the failure. As long as a goodly number recover from a given operation or find some relief from pain or some prolongation of life, we go to the operating table or take our beloved there.

But if spiritual healing is the result of the larger freedom given to God in any human life, we naturally expect God to make a better job of it. "God so loved the world, that he gave his only begotten Son, that whosoever believeth in him should not perish, but have everlasting life." If God is the God of "whosoever," it puzzles us that all who do their best to cooperate with God, in the salvation of body and mind and soul, are not healed.

I began this ministry with a conviction that health and wholeness are God's intentional will for everybody who will meet the conditions. Because I, myself, had been the grateful recipient of God's healing love and power, I had to ask myself some questions about it. There could be no doubt of the healing. The medical records are clear witness to its validity. But why was I healed? Certainly not because I deserved to be healed any more than others who were not healed. After much thought upon the matter, I had to conclude that I was only an illustration of a general possibility. I had to assume that if some are healed and others not, the difference lay not in God's will but in human cooperation or lack of cooperation.

So I began to inquire diligently about the cooperation which we must give if God's will is to be done in us, and for us, and through us. I studied instances of healing. I studied the New Testament. I studied the reports of "healers." My greatest insights resulted when I became newly aware that Jesus associated healing with the manifestation of the kingdom of God, as I wrote in an earlier letter. The kingdom of God is wherever God reigns. God really reigns when we give God free reign in our lives. The changes God suggests and helps to bring about ought therefore to issue not only in essential transformations of character and conduct, but also in physical healing.

Many illnesses are *psychogenic*. They have their origin in wrong emotions and in wrong thinking about self and others and life itself. When God is permitted to supplant fear with confidence, hatred with love, resentment with forgiveness, greed with generosity, guilt with pardon, the many illnesses which these emotions and attitudes have caused should be healed.

Other illnesses are *endogenous*. They have their origin in the physical body. They are the result of germs, viruses, fractures, wounds, harmful foods, malnutrition, etc. Even these diseases are more amenable to treatment if God has been permitted to make one's mental and emotional life what it ought to be.

Nor is this the whole story. God can and does in some instances act directly upon cell and tissue and organ to restore and renew their proper function. Everyone who has studied this area of life with an open mind recognizes the truth of this fact. I remind you of the statement made by Doctor Laidlaw as the result of the studies conducted by our healing seminar: "To the question 'does a healing power exist?' I believe we can answer with an unconditional 'yes.' "

So our big questions still stare us in the face: If God's will is health and God is apparently given a free hand in one's life, why is there often no real healing? And, on the other hand, why is there healing when there is so little evidence that God has been given a free hand?

It seemed to me that there had to be a choice between two hypotheses: Either God was limited by the unfulfilled conditions in the patient's life; or for reasons hidden in the mystery of God it is not God's intentional will that everyone, even the best, should have the glow and joy and power of health.

This letter is already too long, so I must defer till my next the consideration of the hypothesis which I have been led to accept.

A.E.

Letter 10
Human Lives as Channels of God's Healing Power

Dear Phillip,

After confronting the situation described in my last letter, I began operating with the hypothesis that God's intentional will is health for all who will give the necessary cooperation, and that the reason why there is no healing is that the cooperation has not been given; God has not been granted a free hand in the life involved. The person has wanted to use God for healing, rather than to become fit to be used by God in a ministry to others.

I realize that such an accounting may seem to be passing judgment on another person, a thing we ought never to do. But if one is to be helpful to people in this area, one must make some spiritual diagnosis. That is not a judgment. It is just what it implies, an appraisal of the difficulty that prevents God's healing work. It is not a condemnation. It is an offer of help, given that the person may be saved from the ills that afflict and seriously limit that person's life.

This spiritual diagnosis is not always welcomed, any more than the patient always welcomes the revelation that comes in psychological analysis. But if given in love and accepted in humility, it often clears the way for God to impart new life. To that I can offer substantial witness.

I was called into a home where the patient was suffering from a number of different diseases, a list of which the physician had made and which was shown to me. I had answered the call in complete ignorance of the situation. I felt led to ask certain questions, without knowing why I was asking them.

Fortunately, the distressed woman was ready to help discover the reason why she had found no relief through prayer. It soon became evident that she had been greatly wronged, was literally hating the person who had injured her, and felt justified in so doing. It then became a simple matter to let her see that the God of love could not operate in a life that was filled with hatred, that she must forgive to the very core of her being. By the grace of God she did just that, and the result was a new experience of the love and grace of God. When I saw her later she said joyously, "You have brought me new life." Of course God had given her the new life, not I; and together we praised God for the benediction.

Experiences like this have proved over and over again that my hypothesis is at least partly correct. In unmistakable instances healing has not come because the God of love has not been given right of way in the life.

Other experiences have not been so simple. There are people who have, as far as they know, given God the right of way in their lives; but deep in the unconscious there is hidden that which gets in God's way and hinders God's work. It is commonplace, in these days of depth psychology, that people find they do not know themselves. They are surprised and often incredulous as it begins to appear that in the depths of their selfhood there are emotions and attitudes, yearnings and aversions, which their conscious mind disavows. And more often than is recognized, the reason why there is no healing lies right there. Some of the most wonderful healings that I have witnessed have had to wait until there has been an exploration of the unconscious.

There come to mind, as I write, two ministers, both of whom were capable and devoted servants of Christ. One had been ill in bed for a year; the other was a manic-depressive who the psychiatrist said should be hospitalized for a year. Both had been prayed for. Both had prayed for themselves. The childhood experiences of one had been so humiliating that he had become an unwitting perfectionist in the effort to avoid criticism of any kind. He was wearing himself out day by day in parish and pulpit as he strove, without reprieve, to act and speak so that there could be no possible wound to his self-esteem. The other had been retired from his life-long vocation. In his retirement he had been given a position which provided him a satisfying feeling of usefulness. When it was withdrawn he outwardly accepted the situation with grace, but great resentment found a place in his deeper self and was literally breaking his heart.

Both patients were helped to discover what lay buried beneath the conscious level. They both turned God loose on those levels, and healing quickly came. The life and power of the kingdom arrived when they let God reign in areas from which God

69

had been excluded. Something like this is the condition of many people who come for healing. The conscious self may be penitent, forgiving, trusting, humble; the unconscious self may be exactly the opposite. God may reign in the conscious, while self is on the throne in the unconscious.

Such instances again seem to verify my hypothesis; namely, that *God's intentional will is health for everyone and, if prayers for healing are not effective, it is not because God is unwilling, but because God is not given a free hand. In the most sincere, the most consciously dedicated person, there may be unconscious blockages. If those blockages are lifted into consciousness and removed, health comes again.*

But about the time I began to feel confident that the reason for failures was not in the reluctance of God, but in the inner life of the patient, some other facts pressed for attention.

One of those facts is the multiplicity of healings recorded in the ministry of Jesus. "He healed them all" is the statement made more than once. Those "all" were not picked prospects. They certainly could not all have been near-saints or even psychologically integrated persons. Obviously there was no opportunity for long counseling in an effort to uncover the depths and remove any blockages that might exist there. Apparently they were run-of-the-mill men and women, such as might be found in a mass meeting anywhere today.

In some cases Jesus called for faith as a condition of healing. In one instance he first attended to a

man's sins before he could say "Rise up and walk."
In another, he warned one who had been healed,
"Go thy way, and sin no more, lest a worse thing
happen to thee." He asked one cripple, "Do you
really want to be healed?" as if he suspected that
the man might be hugging his invalidism to his
bosom, perhaps as an escape from responsibility.
Some students believe that Jesus took some time
with the Gadarene demoniac before he could set
him free from his inner torments.

But for the most part, at least as far as the records go, Jesus was able to bring health to all sorts of
people who must have had the same limitations
that baffle us today. There was a universality about
his ministry of healing that seems to make our
hypothesis inadequate.

What then? It may be that we shall have to revise
our hypothesis to read something like this: *The
power of the kingdom, in the life of one in whom God
reigns and has a free hand, may operate directly
upon another who is ill even though that other person is not yet wholly committed to God.* That seems
to be what happened to Jesus. He was a kingdom
man. His will was "to do the will of God in heaven."
If ever God reigned without a rival in a human
being, it was in the life of Jesus of Nazareth. So the
power of the kingdom, which is the power of God,
operated in him and through him upon the lives of
others.

I have observed the same power operate through
the lives of a few others. One of the most remarkable experiences I have ever had in the course of my

71

researches in the field of spiritual healing came not long ago. For three hours I sat in a congregation of twelve hundred worshipping people while many sick in the company were healed of various severe illnesses. Some of them came forward for prayer. Others were healed where they sat and then came forward to witness to what had happened and to offer convincing proof of the healing event.

The ministrant refused to take any credit for the healing. She did not even know that the healed were there in the audience until they came with their testimony. Over and over again the ministrant said: "This is God. I did not touch this person. I did not pray for him (or her). This is God." And the ministrant's eyes shone with the same wonder as that which stirred in our hearts. The ministrant is a dedicated woman. Through a friend who had the privilege of three days of companionship with that ministrant, I know that her life is a life of commitment to what she believes is the will of God. She has paid the price in self-discipline that her life might be the scene of the operation of the kingdom of God.

There have been others who seemed to possess what has been called the gift of healing. Paul wrote of such a gift, and it seems to have been among the charismatic experiences which came to some in the church of that day. I have known a few who at times appeared to be the channels through whom the healing power of the kingdom touched the souls and bodies of some who came to them. But the gift did not seem to be universally effective. Some were healed and some "went sadly away."

So my revised hypothesis seems to have some real corroboration.

A.E.

Letter 11
The Mystery of the Healing Power

Dear Phillip,

Thank you for your kind word of appreciation of the two hypotheses which I suggested as to the reasons why some people are healed and others are not. Thank you even more for your suggestion of another hypothesis which might offer an explanation of the ups and downs of spiritual healing and provide a working basis for a healing ministry.

As I understand it, you are saying that we must think in terms of the sovereignty of God. You are ready to affirm that God can and does heal both mental and physical disease. You see God's hand in the healing energy of the body itself, in the researches and discoveries of scientists, and in the application of those discoveries, through *materia medica* and surgery and psychiatry, to our illnesses.

You also feel very strongly that communion with God through prayer and obedience creates a morale in which all therapies are more effective. Finally, you agree that evidence is very convincing that God can and does operate directly upon a sick person and the sickness to effect cures not otherwise possible.

But you wonder if we can ever hope to understand why such cures are so rare; why sometimes the healing passes by people who by their manner of life seem to be the most likely prospects, but is given to others who grant God very little place in their plans and actions. You remind me that we need to keep reminding ourselves that God is God and not human; that mystery must confront the finite in our attempts to comprehend the ways of the infinite; that we must simply trust God's love and wisdom to grant healing or refuse it, and ask no questions about it.

I readily grant your proposal as one way to resolve our dilemmas. Surely it behooves mortals to be very humble in our relationship with God and in our effort to understand God's ways with us. I much relish the criticism made of one very great theologian: "For one who insists that speculation is to be resisted, he gives extremely detailed accounts of the inner life of God." Unhappy indeed the theologian or layperson who presumes to say exactly what God does and how God does it!

But we need to remember that the unwillingness to ask questions may be as presumptuous as asking them. The not asking is often an assumption of knowing what is often not true about God. Ministers in Hanover, New Hampshire, stood by the graves of children who died as infants and chided those who questioned the providence of God in these premature deaths. Their assumption was that these deaths were the will of God. But some who questioned, then and since, determined to explore the real situation. They discovered that these deaths were not the will of God, but a devastation by germs. Those germs were hunted out and destroyed. God was freed of blame and infants no longer are abandoned to what was blasphemously called the will of God.

I find it impossible to believe that cancer and angina pectoris and rheumatoid arthritis, with all their torture and their devastation of homes and their orphaning of children and their termination of useful lives, are the will of God. They have other causes, and we must seek out and remove those causes.

I think we can count on God's help in conquering these terrible enemies of life. That help will be given to scientists, as far as they will allow it, and to sensitive physicians in daily contact with persons who are afflicted. I believe it will also be given to some who are seriously seeking to be the channels of God's direct healing power. I have seen God thus at work and know that God can act beyond the limits of our power to act, and to heal where we scarcely dare to hope for healing.

I have been both surprised and baffled in this area. But I am never so paralyzed by negative experiences that I am unable to pray for those for whom hope has been abandoned, or for illnesses which physicians have pronounced incurable. There is something that has happened to me in my fellowship with God and in my quest for God's will that keeps me yearning to pray for, and with, everyone who asks for help, even when the case has the desperation that surrounds cancer.

So you may guess that I find it impossible to assume that healings are a matter of divine decree which, for no apparent reason, selects some for restoration and abandons others to the ravages of crippling or fatal disease. I cannot but believe that God's will includes every one in its provision and its mercy; that sin and sickness belong to the kingdom of evil and that the kingdom of God seeks to destroy that kingdom wherever it invades human life; that if there is neither holiness nor health, it is not because God is indifferent or uncaring, but that humanity and its personal way of life and its social institutions hinder the saving, healing work of God.

I confess that once and again I am puzzled by what happens or does not happen in the life of any man or woman who appeals for help. But *I am much more ready to believe that the patient is consciously or unconsciously failing to let God in, or that there is something in me that will not let God through to the patient, than I am to assume that God is not interested or that God's interest commits God to a flat refusal to heal.*

I find, too, that people are much more reconciled to failure in the healing effort if I have explained to them that God is doing the best at every moment and that any failure is the result of our failure (theirs and mine) to clear the way for God. Nor do they have a sense of guilt as a result.

They are prompted to keep on searching themselves to find the obstacle even as I likewise search myself. We work as partners who are trying to give God the necessary cooperation. We do not end blaming God if the result is not what we sought. We do accept the fact of our human frailty and rejoice in the fact of God's concern and effort to deliver. We think of God as in the struggle with us, a comrade in the quest, who does not upbraid our frailty but keeps on loving us and enlightening us and turning our apparent defeat into a victory of faith and a stimulus to growth in love for the Creator of all things.

I never assure a person that God will heal. I do share my faith that God wants to heal. I summon the person to join with me in opening the way for God into every area of our lives. This brings us closer to each other and to God and becomes, with exciting results, a joint pilgrimage into the heights and depths of the everlasting mercy.

And when after days or weeks of prayer and counsel, the sick one sometimes descends into the valley of the shadow, our experience together becomes an epic of splendor. God seems so near and so real. All fear is gone. The family is called in for loving communion with each other about "life, death, and that vast forever." Counsel is given for those who are to be left behind. A final kiss, a lingering smile, a wave of the hand, and all is still as the hush of eternity enters the room. It is as beautiful as a voiceless sunset, as awesome as a breath-taking epiphany, as holy as a visitation from the skies. The deathbed has become an altar; the bereaved, a fellowship of worshippers. Heaven has sealed our prayers and our farewells with its own incomparable benediction.

As I look back upon my long life in the ministry, I must confess that the times when God has seemed most near and God's grace most blessed have not always been when someone has been healed of sickness, but in the hours when there was no healing but that of the spirit. Then came a glory that transcended all our hopes, and an assurance that death itself could not dilute or destroy.

So as yet I have no alternative but to continue to teach and pray as if God's intention for us all is health and holiness and wholeness, if we let God reign in our hearts and lives. Anything less than that seems to me to malign God and to fail humanity.

There are not a few persons who find it difficult to live with mystery and to accept the arrival of new questions; but, as one has said, "The postulate of all scholarly investigation is the nagging experience of mystery." As we explore the wider possibilities of spiritual healing and encounter questions for which as yet there is no answer, we must remember that any investigation worthy the name will be confronted by mystery.

Those who are looking for pat answers will be impatient and irresolute. Or they will set up answers which convince nobody but the credulous. Only those who believe in a Christlike God and who are scrupulously honest and persistently intelligent may hope to find increasingly satisfying answers. The answers will not banish all mystery, but they will honor the God involved in the mystery and will help men and women to an ever-growing comprehension and experience of God's love and power.

Of this much we are certain: some for whom we pray will experience a physical healing which could not otherwise have been their happy lot; others will enter into a blessed, conscious comradeship with God; and all will know that the church and its ministers deeply care for them, feel their pains, share their griefs. The church will become "a fellowship of those who bear the mark of pain," which is, strangely enough, a fellowship of unique joy.

A.E.

Letter 12
Relevance of Prayer to Healing

Dear Phillip,

One of the assurances that has made our correspondence a searching yet joyous dialogue is that we both have an abiding concern for the social significance of the kingdom of God. Concern for spiritual healing should not make one indifferent to the social ills which need remedy. We are both committed to the effort to release the spirit and power of the kingdom into the laws and institutions of society. We find it difficult to understand those individuals who insist that the church should be silent in the presence of racial injustice, industrial exploitation, or political betrayal of the commonwealth.

Certainly our own ministry to the sick has not been an escape from the struggles which are involved in the long search for a cure for the maladies of a sick society. We, therefore, have been able to give serious thought to the ministry of individual healing without any sense of betrayal of our social responsibility. In praying "Thy kingdom come," we really mean exactly that. It is our purpose to seek first the kingdom in all its relevance to human life, individually and socially. We want God to reign everywhere! To the establishment of that reign we are committed with whatever we have to offer God that will hasten its fulfillment.

That commitment has as great significance for

our prayers as for our action. Jesus believed that prayer is one of the significant offerings we can bring to God's victory. But it must be not self-centered but kingdom-centered prayer—prayer that does not seek to use God for one's egocentric purposes, but prayer that one may become the kind of person God can use for the kingdom's purposes, which are born in wisdom and love.

When we come to God for healing either for ourselves or for others, the decisive questions, it seems to me are: Why is healing wanted? Merely to get rid of pain? Merely to prolong life? Merely to enable one to pursue more vigorously earthly aims and ambitions? Merely to save medical expenses and so have more to spend on conspicuous consumption or exciting diversion?

If healing comes, will there be a grateful dedication to God and to one's fellow human beings? Will the renewal of physical energy result in a more energetic devotion to spiritual quests? Will the world have a better understanding of God's will for human life? Will anyone sing to God with new fervor, "How great thou art"? Will life become not easier, but more heroic? If healing comes, will it make one more compassionate and more concerned to abolish the poverty and the injustice which are breeding grounds for the illnesses which afflict so many? If healing comes, will the restoration of health make one more concerned for the health of others?

Too often prayers for healing are prayers not for the kingdom of God but for the kingdoms of earth!

They set humanity, its ambitions, greed, rivalries, ease, and dusty success at the center. God and divine purity, holiness, love, and power are on the periphery; and even there only as accessories.

In that kind of prayer I cannot join. Nor can I think of prayer as a means of persuading God to do what God otherwise would not do, or not to do what God was bent on doing. If God is not concerned with the health of a person, my prayers are not going to waken any concern in the divine consciousness. If God is concerned but reluctant to use power to heal, my prayers will not overcome the divine reluctance. As I see it, prayer's relation to healing is as our response to God's will for health and our cooperation with that will in begetting health. Prayer is opening ourselves to the God who in Jesus Christ has demonstrated concern for the abundant life of God's own people.

God is the ever present source of life, giving that source to us just as much as we will permit. God is the love that will not let us go, the light that follows all the way, the joy that seeks us through pain; and even as we bear our cross God is lifting up our heads with the promise of endless life. In true prayer we respond to that love, we open our eyes to that light, we accept the joy that comes through pain, we take our cross and let it lift us above the dust of our self-concern.

God is present wherever we are, whatever our plight. God is a part of every breath we draw, every cry of pain that escapes our lips, every plea for deliverance from crippling disease. Without God

85

we could not breathe, nor cry, nor plead. God is here as the oxygen that answers to our need for breath, as the surcease of the pain that evokes the cry, as the deliverance that turns the plea into praise.

The purpose of prayer is to open our whole selves to divine intervention; to grant God a welcome beyond the limits of our mere existential relationship; to invite God to be to us more than a bare necessity of our very existence; to give God "the freedom of the city," the key to all that we are and all that we may become by heavenly action upon our willingness.

True prayer is the opening of our *minds* to the divine consciousness, by relinquishing our prejudices, our prepossessions, our absorption in things, our pet fads and fancies, our fondly cherished illusions, our habitual ways of thinking; and by responding to the hints, the cautions, the challenges, the corrections which God's spirit brings to the threshold of consciousness.

True prayer is the opening of our *hearts* to the divine presence by renouncing our petty affections, our juvenile aversions, our adult passions and resentments, our socially conditioned fears and frenzies, all of which hamper God's effort to help and to heal. In true prayer there is always a housecleaning, an examination of self in the light of Christ, a "change of heart."

True prayer is an opening of our *wills* to God. Tennyson said it memorably:

> Our wills are ours, we know not how;
> Our wills are ours, to make them thine.[9]

Always to pray realistically "Thy kingdom come" is to add "Thy will be done." Prayer that is a demand upon God is madness. What is needed always is the spirit of Dame Gertrude More: "Be Thou . . . my chooser for me, for Thou art my only choice."[10]

Therefore, true prayer sets God free in a human life. It does not persuade God to heal. It permits God to do what is necessary to any real healing of disease of the body and mind and spirit.

In that spirit, Phillip, I will offer my prayers for you and your efforts to bring health to God's people. In that spirit let us both pray for the church that it may be truly apostolic in its proclamation of the gospel of our risen Lord.

Forever yours in the love of Christ,

A.E.

Study Guide

Letter 1: The Question of Involvement in Spiritual Healing

1. "Should I undertake a healing ministry?" The author calls this "the big question." Perhaps you should answer a preliminary question before dealing with the big question: "What in my life causes me to be interested in a healing ministry?"

Take a few moments to reflect on this question. You may want to consider names of persons, events, places, and some of your own personal questions that are motivating your interest in the healing ministry. Share your reflections with the other group members.

2. Many Christians hesitate to get involved in "spiritual healing" because of negative experiences such as fanaticism related to some healing services, unsubstantiated claims by healers, and the disillusionment of empty promises. It may be helpful in your group-building process to take whatever time is needed to share negative experiences or personal doubts about spiritual healing. People usually have questions, reservations, and biases about this controversial topic. Allow your group to grant permission in these sessions to express personal feelings without fear of condemnation and criticism.

3. Have you ever prayed "with great earnestness for healing" for yourself or another person with no apparent relief? How did that leave you feeling? What questions and issues about healing or the lack of healing did this experience raise?

4. Close this session with silent prayer and re-flection. Then, invite each one in the group to join in unison prayer:

Spirit of the living God, whose healing presence we now seek and claim, we lift up to you
    our questions and answers,
    our doubts and affirmations,
    our stories of failures as well as successes.
As we covenant together,
    may we learn from one another,
    may we be totally receptive to your wisdom and
        insights,
    may we eventually emerge with a better under-standing of your gracious healing ministry,
    and in this learning, growing process, grant each
        of us wholeness in body, mind, spirit, and in all
        our relationships. In the name of Jesus Christ,
        Amen.

Letter 2: Contradiction and Paradox

1. The author suggests that when health is restored, "It is not a simple matter to determine where the credit belongs."

Can you name someone who you feel was healed by spiritual means such as prayer, faith, sacraments, or Biblical teachings? Describe the circumstances.

Can you name someone who you feel was healed by other means such as medicine, doctor's treatments, patient's will to live, the body's ability to heal itself? Describe the circumstances.

Consider the possibility that God uses many different kinds of therapy to help and to heal people. Discuss the implications of this idea.

2. Although the relevance of prayer to healing is later presented in Letter 12, it might be appropriate at this point to consider your understanding of prayer as compared to the author's, who might define "right prayer" as fellowship with Christ that engenders trust, fosters the body's own therapeutic activity, challenges the condition that produces the illness, and purges the emotions of worry, hate, resentment, anxiety, and jealousy.

Suggest your own definition of "right prayer." Share.

3. The healing ministry of Jesus receives much space in all four Gospel accounts. Have the group read some of these healing incidents and then reflect together. Use Appendix One in this book to

identify these passages. After reading, either silently or aloud, describe the illness or problem in
writing and identify the factors that contributed to
the healing.

4. Invite discussion, as time permits, on other
questions and issues arising from your study of
Letter 2. One example might be the author's struggles and apparent helplessness over his wife's suffering with rheumatoid arthritis.

5. Close with prayer.

Letter 3: Evidence for the Reality
of Spiritual Healing

1. Rather than starting with a negative viewpoint, the author strongly suggests a positive approach. Three sources of evidence for genuine spiritual healing are listed: accounts of healing in the four Gospels (see Appendix One), medical bureau records at Lourdes, France, and published reports by health professionals in the United States. Discuss these three kinds of evidence.

2. Dr. Laidlaw states, "Does a healing power exist? I believe we can answer with an unconditional 'yes.' " Does anyone in the group have personal experiences or other kinds of contemporary evidence that point to a healing power or a healing force in the universe? Listen and share with open minds.

3. If illustrations of healing by spiritual means are shared in the group, continue the positive approach by asking, "What were the conditions that favored success?" Write down these factors and keep for reference. You may want to keep a personal journal documenting various evidences of healing.

4. Not all can take penicillin; not all can take aspirin. An effective physician does not give each patient the same prescription. Are we sometimes guilty of using or prescribing the same spiritual therapy for all persons? Discuss.

You may want to add to the list of various kinds of spiritual therapy: Holy Communion, private and group prayer, laying on of hands with prayer, anointing with oil and prayer, fasting, Bible reading, memorizing certain scripture passages, silent meditation, Christian counseling, reading biographies and writings of the saints.

5. What is the most significant insight you had this week? Share.

6. Close with prayer.

Letter 4: The Kingdom of God— Source of Healing Power

1. Seven factors are identifiable in any healing process: the life-force within the body itself; the will-to-live of the patient; the meaningfulness the patient has found in life which gives an urgency to go on living; the patient's faith in God and the attending physician; the sense of being loved and needed; the medicines prescribed; and the physiotherapy employed. The group may want to discuss one or more of these factors.

Compare this list to the one compiled in response to question 3 in the guide for reflection and discussion related to Letter 3.

2. The kingdom of God, according to Jesus, is the source from which comes life and healing power. Take three minutes to write out your definition of the kingdom of God. Have each group member read what was written to the group. Discuss and compare these to the author's definition of the kingdom of God: "wherever God reigns."

3. The author stimulates our thinking with these contrasting statements about the gospel of spiritual healing.

Is Not	Is
An offer of cheap grace	An offer of grace sufficient
Immunity from life	Ability for life

Is Not	Is
An excuse for ignorance of nature's laws or defiance of these laws	An insight into the role of nature's laws and a mastery of those laws
Immunity from temptation and disease	An ever present possibility of victory over temptation and disease
Earned or deserved	A gift of health and sanctity

Your group may want to add to the "is not" and "is" columns.

4. Spiritual healing, according to the author, is "one manifestation of the power and life and holiness of God. It is the result of the individual actively being open in every area of being to the reign of God. That result may be aided by those who have admitted God to the throne of their own lives and who, by reason of that fact, become allies of God on the one hand and on the other hand the helpers of those who are trying to learn how to admit God to rule in their lives to heal sickness, purify the heart, illuminate the mind, and energize the will."

Read this aloud in the group. Take one minute to reflect silently. Then discuss this definition of spiritual healing.

5. Close with prayer.

Letter 5: The God of the Kingdom

1. God is indescribable, yet most of us have personal ideas about God's being. When you pray, how do you "visualize" God? When you think "God," what images and ideas come to mind? Write down some of these and share them with the group. You may want to compare your understanding of God with that of the author.

2. Can you identify with the author's statement, "In my best moments I feel at home with God"? Can you name and describe some of those "best moments" in your life when you do feel at home with God?

3. Name some ways we can give God our consent and our cooperation realizing, as the author states, "God will not reign, God cannot reign, without my consent; yes, without my cooperation. Given that consent and cooperation, new and otherwise impossible events begin to happen—illumination, conquest over temptation, healing for the body."

4. Discuss the author's concept of "poverty of expectation." Do we limit God's power and action in our lives by expecting too much from ourselves and by not expecting more from God? Name and share some examples from your own life when you had "poverty of expectation."

5. The author repeatedly emphasizes the healing

action of God in and through human beings, especially health professionals. "The chemist, the physician, the surgeon, the psychiatrist are working with God if they are working effectively for the sake of health." Have the group discuss this concept further.

6. Share the most exciting insight that came to you this week.

7. Join in this meditation for closing. The author declares, "real spiritual healing depends" on the enthronement of God in the lives of men and women.

In a moment of quietness, remove everything from your hands, and your lap. With feet on the floor, get as comfortable as you can and visualize in your imagination an empty throne. This empty throne symbolizes the center of your personal life, the very heart of your being. Whoever sits on this throne directly controls your life.

Ask this question, with your eyes closed and concentrating on that empty throne of your life: "Who sits on the throne of my life most often?"

If you feel led, take this opportunity to invite the God of heaven and earth,

the God who created you,
the God who redeems you,
the God who sustains you,

to be seated on the throne of your life. Take several moments to contemplate this decision and action.

Remember, God will not reign, God cannot reign

without your consent and your cooperation. Remember, also, that you can always intentionally invite the God of the kingdom to sit on the throne of your personal life anytime or anywhere you may be.

Pray aloud, in unison, the Lord's Prayer, being especially sensitive to references to the kingdom. The group may want to stand in a circle, holding hands, for this concluding prayer.

Letter 6: Jesus' Concept of the Kingdom—
Charter for Spiritual Healing

1. The kingdom of God means the reign of God. This means God having the right of way in one's life, one's thinking, one's choosing, one's acting. Work through this exercise as it may apply to you.

My life: Is there an area of my life where God does not have the right of way? Reflect.
My thinking: Do I have some thoughts and ideas that need to be under God's control? Reflect.
My choosing: Am I facing some choices and decisions that call for divine guidance? Reflect.
My actions: Is my behavior reflecting God's reign or self reign? Reflect.

2. The kingdom of God or the reign of God as related to true spiritual healing, states the author, is convincing, enlightening, and thrilling. One of the greatest claims of Jesus is that human beings can begin to live in God's kingdom now.
Recall some recent events, places, persons you have experienced that have thrilled you, enlightened you, and convinced you of the reality of the kingdom of God now. Share with the other group members.

3. Name and describe some of your "little dukedoms" that sometimes get first place priority in your life, even to the extent of crowding out God's great kingdom. This may be more difficult to do.

4. The gift of health, wholeness, and salvation is

one of the great benedictions (signs) of God's kingdom breaking through in human lives. Jesus taught and demonstrated this again and again. The author paraphrased Jesus' reply to John's followers (Matt. 11:2-6): The objective of the kingdom is "the healing of men's diseases, the forgiveness of sins, the conquest of human hearts, the illumination of minds, the creation of a fellowship of love. This is already being achieved. Blessed is the person who does not lose faith in me and in the kingdom!"

This may be a new concept for some. Do you associate those times when you have experienced healing, forgiveness, illumination, and love with signs of God's kingdom in your life? Discuss.

5. Reflect on the author's "charter for a ministry to the sick": Health is a concern of the kingdom of God; The God of the kingdom can and does act in behalf of health and wholeness; Christians are not only authorized to dedicate themselves to the healing of sickness, but also to count upon and to call upon the help of God in such an undertaking. Could it be, as the author suggests, that acceptance of such a charter with full understanding of its meaning will save us from the misconception that often eats into the adventure of spiritual healing? Discuss.

6. Close with prayer.

Letter 7: Membership in the Kingdom— the Condition of Healing

1. Let us begin with the author's summary statement: "God can and does heal where God is permitted to reign. Our responsibility is to offer the throne in our lives to God."

The strong suggestion is that the conditions of healing are the same as those which determine our entrance into the kingdom and its entrance into us. "The prime condition for healing is to enter the kingdom, to let God reign, to give God a free hand in one's life." Perhaps this is a new idea for you. Think it through right now, especially as it relates to prayers for healing.

When you pray for the healing of another person or for yourself, how would you pray if you took seriously the condition of healing as stated above? Reflect on this, and discuss it with the group. Then, in silence, visualize one of your friends or family members who needs wholeness and healing in body, mind, spirit, or relationships. Write out a brief prayer of intercession based on "the condition of healing."

2. Have you ever met someone who said, "I am not good enough to expect God to heal me"? If so, how did you respond?

3. Do you sometimes have difficulty praying for yourself? Some of us labor under the self-imposed burden that we must earn or deserve God's healing love. If healing depended upon an adequate good-

104

ness on our part, there would be no healing of anybody anywhere. Adequate goodness is not a condition of healing. Discuss this in the group.

4. Silently reflect on these questions:

Am I guilty of declaring my intention, but not really surrendering my throne to God?

Have I announced my engagement with the Lord, but never followed through with deep bonds of unity?

Is self still on my throne with God being permitted only an advisory function now and then?

Ask each one in the group to pray aloud the prayer written in the first question. At the conclusion of each prayer, have the group respond in unison: "Thank you, Lord, for helping and healing."

After these prayers have been given, pray the Lord's Prayer together.

Letter 8: Nature of Membership in the Kingdom

1. The author suggests that some persons pretend that God is on the throne of their lives, but because God does not actually reign in their minds and hearts, the healing for which they pray does not take place. How do you respond to this statement? Discuss.

2. The author suggests that to have God actually reign in a human life is to will to have God's will as the final authority.

Think of several of the decisions you are facing today and in the days ahead. Are you actively seeking God's will for guidance and final authority in each situation? Perhaps the author's checklist will help clarify. To will to have God's will as the final authority:

Does not mean	Does mean
The striving for an absurd moral perfection	An earnest, genuine, ceaselessly renewed moral intention
Strain, stress, fret, and anxiety	A joyful trusting of God's wisdom, love, and power
Grim, glum, and gritty enslavement to the minutiae of life	An every-morning-awaiting-new-light-from-heaven on the day's tasks

Does not mean	Does mean
Self-reliance	A continuing inquiry, "What will thou have me to do?"

What would you add to the author's checklist?

3. Imagine for a few moments what your life would be like, feel like, and look like if God were actually reigning on the throne of your life every minute of every hour.

4. Are you bold enough to pray for your fantasy of God reigning 100 percent in your life to come true in this life? Reflect on this silently and, if you will, pray for it fervently. The God of the kingdom proclaims, "Behold, I make all things new." All of this is intimately related to the gospel of healing.

1. The question is asked, "Why are the healings comparatively few in comparison with the many (persons) who are not healed?"

A human tendency is to rationalize what seems to be failure in healing. Sometimes we hear, "Our prayers were answered. He is now healed permanently via death." Or, some would lay all responsibility for failure on the person for whom prayer was offered, suggesting, "lack of faith," "hidden sin," or "an inner rebellion." What are some ways you rationalize or deal with apparent failure in healing? Have you discovered some insights that have been helpful to you? Discuss.

2. This letter, rather than presenting new ideas or new directions, repeats several of the author's major concepts. Before proceeding, take a time-out to check where we have been and where we are now. These questions help to sum up the essence of Letter 9:

Where are you in your understanding of Albert Day's approach to spiritual healing?

Where are you regarding your own understanding of spiritual healing?

What has been helpful and enlightening in this book and in your reflections so far?

What continues to puzzle and perplex you?

What are some other issues and questions you might like to raise in the group?

3. Close with prayer.

Letter 10: Human Lives as Channels of God's Healing Power

1. "God's intentional will is health for all who will give the necessary cooperation, and that the reason why there is no healing is that the cooperation has not been given. God has not been granted a free hand in the life involved." Discuss the strengths and weaknesses of the author's original theory of healing.

2. "The power of the kingdom, in the life of one in whom God reigns and has a free hand, may operate directly upon another who is ill even though that other person is not yet wholly committed to God." Discuss the strengths and weaknesses of the author's revised theory.

3. The author's revised theory of healing is patterned after Jesus' healing ministry. "The power of the kingdom operated in [Jesus] and through him upon the lives of others." Can you recall persons, events, situations when the power of the kingdom operated in a Christian and through that Christian upon the lives of others? Consider these instances.
   What are the implications for prayer groups who pray for others (intercessory prayer)? Discuss.

4. First Corinthians 12:9 names "gifts of healing" along with other gifts of the Spirit. Perhaps you have known Christians who were gifted with certain gifts of healing. Notice the author, while claiming authenticity for charismatic experiences,

also states that he has only known a few such gifted Christians and that gifts of healing did not seem to be universally effective.

It is also evident, when examining the data on effectiveness in healing, that some people are healed by and through those who claim no apparent gifts of healing. Discuss this situation.

5. Are you now ready to "spell out" your own theory of healing? Your own philosophy or hypothesis of healing? This may take some unhurried time and prayer. You may want to do this privately, then share what you have written at your next group session.

6. Close with prayer.

Letter 11: The Mystery of the Healing Power

1. In this letter the author acknowledges another explanation of the ups and downs of spiritual healing. Based on the sovereignty of God (the majestic mystery of God), this theory states that God is God, that ultimately human beings cannot understand or explain the mystery of the will of God; therefore, our role is simply to trust God's love and God's wisdom to grant healing or to refuse healing, and ask no questions about it. How do you feel about this "trust-accept-ask no questions" hypothesis of healing? Discuss.

2. The previous statement is one way to resolve our dilemmas. But the author writes, "I am never so paralyzed by negative experiences that I am unable to pray for those for whom hope has been abandoned, or for illnesses which physicians have pronounced incurable. There is something that has happened to me in my fellowship with God and in my quest for God's will that keeps me yearning to pray for, and with, everyone who asks for help, even when the case has the desperation that surrounds cancer."
Have someone in the group read aloud the above statement. Silently reflect a few moments, then discuss.

3. "As I look back upon my long life in the ministry, I must confess that the times when God has seemed most near and God's grace most blessed have not always been when someone has been healed of sick-

ness, but in the hours when there was no healing but that of the spirit. Then came a glory that transcended all our hopes, and an assurance that death itself could not dilute or destroy." Ponder and discuss these related issues:

Have you experienced a "glory that transcended all our hopes, and an assurance that death itself could not dilute or destroy"?

What is the role of death in the healing process?

Physically, all human beings are terminal. What are some of the reasons many people seem to repress or try to ignore this fact? Discuss several.

What do you suppose the author means by "healing of the spirit"?

4. What are some other issues and questions raised in your consciousness by this letter on the mystery of the healing power?

5. From your study of this particular letter have you gained any new ideas or helpful insights? Relate them and discuss.

6. Close with prayer.

Letter 12: Relevance of Prayer to Healing

1. Examine, for a moment, your personal prayers. Have you ever made demands upon God? Have there been occasions when you have tried to use prayer to persuade God to do what God otherwise would not do or not to do what God was already doing? Have you sometimes, in praying for healing, offered prayers to enhance the kingdom of self rather than to cooperate with the kingdom of God? After reflecting on these questions, discuss the implications of prayer as making demands upon God.

2. "Prayer's relation to healing is as our response to God's will for health and our cooperation with that will in begetting health. Prayer is opening ourselves to the God who in Jesus Christ has demonstrated concern for the abundant life of God's own people." Discuss this statement by the author.

3. The author would define true prayer as the opening of our minds, hearts, and wills to God, the opening of our whole selves to God; as granting God a welcome beyond the limits of mere existential relationship to God; as inviting God to be to us more than a bare necessity of our very existence; as giving God "the freedom of the city," the key to all that we are and all that we may become by God's action upon our willingness.

Write in a sentence or two your understanding of authentic or true prayer. Discuss this, comparing your definitions to the author's.

4. Take as much time as needed in the group to deal with these questions:

Do you see any connection between ministry to unhealthy persons and ministry to a sick society?

When you pray "Thy kingdom come," do you envision the salvation and wholeness of communities and nations as well as the healthiness of individual persons?

Does the gospel of healing as taught and demonstrated by Jesus have anything to do with minority and racial injustices, with the political systems that govern us, with the exploitation of human beings as "things," and with the prostitution of the earth and its resources?

5. Review your notes at the end of each letter. If you are meeting with a group, do this before you meet. Discuss what seems to be appropriate for you in each of the following topics:

On what questions and issues related to the healing ministry are you awaiting and seeking further light?

What insights, new thoughts, and exciting ideas have come to you in the reading, studying, and reflecting on this book?

What is the next step I could take in becoming more active and more intentional in Christ's healing ministry today?

6. When Christians share their struggles and their joys over a period of several weeks in a small group setting, the spirit of Christ is experienced in

114

many ways. You may want to conclude your time together by inviting each one in the group to express personal appreciation and affirmation of each other. Be specific. Be yourself. Close with prayers of thanksgiving, gratitude, wholeness, and commitment to the healing Christ.

APPENDIX ONE
The Scriptures and Healing

Insight concerning spiritual healing is greatly enhanced by a thorough knowledge of the holy scriptures. Faith is strengthened as heart and mind become saturated with the written word. This will lead to a better understanding of the living Word, Jesus Christ, and how he heals today. This is a complete listing of healings in the New Testament and a partial listing of references to healing in the Old Testament. Carefully read, study, and meditate on these passages.

Individual Healings by Jesus

	Matthew	Mark	Luke	John
1. Nobleman's son				4:46-54
2. Unclean spirit		1:21-29	4:31-37	
3. Simon's mother-in-law	8:14-15	1:29-31	4:38-39	
4. A leper	8:1-4	1:4-45	5:12-16	
5. Paralytic carried by four	9:1-9	2:1-12	5:17-26	
6. Sick man at the pool				5:2-18
7. Withered hand	12:9-14	3:1-6	6:6-11	
8. Centurian's servant	8:5-13		7:2-10	
9. Widow's son raised			7:11-17	
10. Demoniac (s) at Gadara	8:28-34	5:1-20	8:26-36	
11. Issue of blood	9:20-22	5:25-34	8:43-48	
12. Jairus's daughter raised	9:18-26	5:21-43	8:40-56	
13. Two blind men	9:27-31			
14. Dumb devil possessed	9:32-34			
15. Daughter of Canaan woman	15:21-28	7:24-30		
16. Deaf, speech impediment		7:32-37		
17. Blind man of Bethsaida		8:22-26		
18. Epileptic boy	17:14-21	9:14-29	9:37-42	
19. Man born blind				9:1-14
20. Man blind, deaf, possessed	12:22-30		11:14-26	
21. Woman bent double			13:10-17	
22. Man with dropsy			14:1-5	
23. Raising of Lazarus				11:1-44
24. Ten lepers			17:11-19	
25. Blind Bartimaeus	20:29-34	10:45-52	18:35-43	

Multiple Healings by Jesus

	Matthew	Mark	Luke	John
1. Crowd at Peter's door	8:6-17	1:32-34	4:40-41	
2. Crowds after leper healed			5:14-16	
3. Crowd near Capernaum	12:15-21	3:7-12	5:17-19	
4. Answering John's question	11:2-6		7:18-23	
5. Before feeding the 5,000	14:13-14		9:11	
6. At Gennesaret	14:34-36	6:53-55		
7. Before feeding 4,000	15:29-31			
8. Crowds beyond the Jordan	19:1-2			
9. Blind & lame in temple	21:14			
10. Some sick of Nazareth	13:53-58	6:1-6		
11. All kinds of sickness	4:23	6:56		
12. Every sickness & disease	9:35			
13. All oppressed (Acts 10:38)				

Individual Healings by the Apostles

	Acts
1. The lame man from birth	3:1-12
2. Paul regains his sight	3:10-22; 22:11-13
3. Aeneas the paralytic	9:32-35
4. Raising of Dorcas	9:36-42
5. Crippled man by Lystra	14:8-18
6. Girl with a spirit of divination	16:16-18
7. Eutychus restored to life	20:7-12
8. Paul healed of snake-bite	28:1-6
9. Father of Publius healed	28:7-8

Multiple Healings by the Apostles

	Acts
1. Many wonders and signs	2:43
2. Many sick healed in Jerusalem	5:12-16
3. Stephen performs many miracles	6:8
4. Philip heals many at Samaria	8:5-13
5. Paul and Barnabas work signs and wonders	14:3
6. Paul heals at Ephesus	19:11-12
7. Sick healed at Melita	28:9

Some Other New Testament Scriptures

1. Instructions of Jesus and promises to believers	Mark 16:14-20, Luke 10:8-9
2. Signs and wonders	Rom. 15:18-19 2 Cor. 12:12, Heb. 2:4
3. Healing	1 Cor. 12:9, 12:28-30

4. Anointing	Mark 6:13, James 5:14
5. Perfect eternal healing	Rev. 21:4

Some Old Testament References
to Healing

1. None of these diseases	Exodus 15:26
2. The fiery serpent	Numbers 21:6-9
3. Schunammite's son raised	II Kings 4:18-37
4. Naaman healed	II Kings 5:1-14
5. Hezekiah healed	II Kings 20:1-11
6. "With His stripes we are healed"	Isaiah 53:5
7. Some healing Psalms	Psalm 23, 30, 103
8. Dead man raised	II Kings 13:20-21

APPENDIX TWO
The Ministry to the Sick

Originally in pamphlet form, this brief essay, containing helpful theology and important principles, set out a basic understanding for Albert E. Day's ministry and later writings.

Dr. Day conducted public healing services in local churches when it was not the accepted thing to do. This essay is an early explanation of his theology of wholeness and the sensitive use of healing principles, which continue to benefit and enlighten the curious and the committed.

A prayer for the spiritual healing of mental or physical illness may be offered by anybody anywhere. The effectiveness of such a prayer will depend in part upon the person who prays and the person for whom the prayer is offered. God is always eager to help and to heal. God needs no persuasion, but God does need our intelligent cooperation.

That cooperation requires of us repentance for our sins and a sincere dedication to the doing of God's holy and loving will. This will is expressed in the laws of hygiene as well as in the moral law, in the therapies which medical science offers as well as in those emotional attitudes which are life-making, and especially in the commandment to love God "with all our heart, soul, strength, and mind" and our neighbors as ourselves. To flout God's will in any of its expressions is to invite disease and to frustrate God's purpose for health.

That does not mean that only perfect people can pray or expect healing. There are no perfect people this side of heaven. It is very doubtful if even those who enter the celestial city will find themselves immediately made perfect in holiness or love. God will still have a lot of unfinished business with all of us. Some cleansing spiritual baths will have to be taken, some rigorous therapies will have to be applied; some surprising lessons in celestial etiquette will have to be learned ere we can join the company of "just men made perfect."

Prayer is not the monopoly of the perfect but a resource ever available to the imperfect. Its real efficiency is proved over and over by those who are discontent with their imperfections and are seriously trying to overcome them. We must not forget that Jesus looked with enthusiasm upon the man who stood with bowed head, keenly conscious of his unworthiness, and prayed, "God be merciful to me a sinner." But we must not forget, either, that the higher reaches of prayer and its greater redemptive power are known only to those who weave the spirit of the Lord's Prayer into every prayer they offer, and who have learned that it is only as we abide in Christ and he abides in us, that the healing of bodies and souls can be expected.

Personal Prayer for the Sick

May you pray for the sick and for yourself when ill? Yes, by all means. But always look carefully to yourself, your way of life, your relationships with

God and your fellow human beings, your fidelity to everyday duties, your selfless concern and compassion for God's other needy children of every race and clan. Are you doing all you can for your own need and for theirs, instead of trying to use God for an errand boy and make God a substitute for your laziness, your thoughtlessness, your self-indulgence? Will you become the kind of person whom God can use not only in healing sick bodies but in winning others to the way of Christ? Instead of asking God to send some angel to heal and redeem, will you say, "Here am I; send me"? And will you keep on loving God even when the answer is delayed or comes not at all in the way you expect it? Will you give God a free hand in your life? Will you quit trying to instruct God but let God tell you? Will you throw away the schedule you have fixed up and let God set the hour and the place for your healing? Will you break out of the deadly circle of preoccupation with yourself and seek God's kingdom, first, last, and all the time? Will you get yourself off your own puny, grasping, trembling hands into God's and leave yourself there, no matter what happens? Can you say, "Yes, Lord, always yes"; "do with me as thou wilt, when thou wilt"?

If the answer to all of these questions is "yes," or "I will try by God's help," then pray on, pray expectantly, pray happily, pray persistently. You will not pray in vain!

Services for Spiritual Healing

While prayers for spiritual healing may be offered by anyone, at any time, anywhere, there are special considerations which must be kept in mind by those who are planning public services where prayers for healing are to be offered. The gospel of healing has been discredited in many places by reason of practices that have entered into this ministry. It is to help avoid anything that may bring this sacred service into disrepute and to encourage those who, in the name of Christ and inspired by his loving concern for the sick, seek to become channels of God's healing power, that these instructions have been prepared.

No Fixed Patterns

There are many patterns for such services, which have grown out of the ecclesiastical traditions of those employing them, or out of the individual minister's experience with the mode which best fits that minister's personality or the temper of the community in which the work takes place. To those to whom the sacraments are especially meaningful, the service of Holy Communion, the anointing with oil, the liturgical prayer seem to be the most helpful in stimulating the essential faith and fostering a sense of the presence of the healing Christ.

To others a simpler form of service with hymns and extemporaneous prayer and the laying on of hands makes the greater appeal and seems to release the greater power.

Some have the sick come to the altar in groups; some insist that they come one by one. Some maintain a profound silence during the ministrations at the altar; others offer such audible prayers as seem inspired by the supplicant's need. Some have a stated service once a week in chapel or sanctuary, believing that this frequency and regularity gives to the community a sense of its importance and encourages people to come because they know just when the prayers will be offered; others have services only once or twice a month. Some make the service as open to the public as the Sunday service of worship; others confine it to less conspicuous places such as a church parlor and make it only a phase of a prayer group experience.

Only a very foolish person would attempt to fix an orthodoxy of practice, or declare that one method is universally better than another, or insist that one pattern is inspired by the Holy Spirit and therefore preferred everywhere.

One Serviceable Method

Many have asked the writer to share the method which he used for seven years in his own pastorate. I do it, not because it is authoritative and final, but just because it may be helpfully suggestive to those who are eager to begin this ministry.

Our service was held in our beautiful chapel with its high altar, its storied windows, its divided chancel and two prie-dieux for kneeling supplicants. We wore pulpit robes, as befits the sacredness of this ministry. The organ played hymns just before the hour while people were assembling. Promptly at eleven on Wednesday the ministrants took their places in the chancel. After a few moments of impressive silence, one of us knelt before the high altar and led the worshippers in the prayer for cleansing. This was followed by the Lord's Prayer and the New Life Hymn, "Breathe on Me Breath of God," which we sang at every service and with which the people became so familiar that they could sing it without the book, thus making it truly a prayer-hymn full of meaning. Then came the special scripture for the day with comments and extemporaneous prayer. After this we always had at least twenty or thirty minutes of teaching, in which we sought to make explicit the New Testament faith in the Saviorhood of Jesus Christ, his concern for the sick, his practice of healing, his commission to his church, the conditions of healing illustrated in his ministry, his relevance to human need. We also interpreted the psychosomatic nature of many illnesses, the impact of childhood traumas upon adult health, the steps necessary to bring the unconscious patterns into harmony with conscious intentions, and many other important truths affecting the human appropriation of divine grace.

Those who desired prayer were then invited to come and kneel one at a time at the prie-dieu where my associate and I stood. They whispered their request to the one waiting to minister to them, hands were laid upon their head and silent prayer was offered in their behalf. At the same time, the worshippers present were asked to pray for the ones kneeling. All this took place amid profound silence, which visitors said was one of the most moving experiences in which they had ever shared. After the last supplicant was again seated, there came the benediction and the end of the public service.

We believe that the laying on of hands was an effective part of this service. There was no suspicion of magic in the practice. Human hands on the worshippers' heads said to them that someone greatly cared for them. That someone was Christ's minister. Maybe Christ, himself, cared, too. At least that seemed to be the impression made. As a result faith was stimulated—and that is always of first rate importance! Also we came to believe, as do many others who practice the laying on of hands, that in some strange but beautiful way God seems to use the consecrated and consecrating hands as conveyors of healing life. Many will testify that in this sacramental relationship as ministers to the sick, they themselves have a sense of power flowing through them to the supplicant. Researchers in this field are trying to invent an instrument that will record and measure this power. Whether they ever succeed or not, it is certain that there is a real sacramental value in this token or symbol of the love and power of God.

We tried the use of anointing oil but as it was foreign to the traditions of our church we found that it was a hindrance rather than a help. Also since our people were not accustomed to the frequent celebration of the Lord's Supper, its observance at this weekly Wednesday service did not contribute as much as it would to people who were trained in other traditions.

Important Principles

Those of us who participated in this service for seven years can witness to its beauty, its dignity, its effectiveness. Whatever the form of service, experience clearly indicates that some principles should be in control.

1. Since it is a service for spiritual healing, *it should be a truly spiritual service*. Any form of religious mumbo jumbo, any attempt to evoke crowd emotion by specious devices known to crowd manipulators, any exploitation of any personality, any exhibitionism or showmanship on the part of the leader, any trickery employed to simulate healings that have not taken place, any extravagant promises given to create unreal hopes, any denunciation of doctors or of practitioners of other faiths should be sedulously avoided. Reverence for God, respect for the truth, love for all humanity should characterize every service. God is the healer and the people should be helped to be aware of God's presence and to look to God for help. They should go away saying, *"what a wonderful Savior,"* rather than exclaiming about the shrewdness or the egocentricity or the magnetism of the speaker.

2. It should be a service for *the explicit teaching of the New Testament faith and practice*. "Faith comes

by hearing and hearing by the word." Much that passes for faith these days is only surmise or wishful thinking or untutored assent to current fads and fancies. The value of a healing service is determined by its effective communication of the truth in Christ. Once a sound foundation is laid in the minds and hearts of people for faith in the healing will of God as revealed in Christ, they are in position not only to lay hold upon God's power for their own health but also to become channels for God's power to the lives of others.

3. Very valuable it will be for *the pastor to communicate some of the truths about ourselves disclosed by sound psychology.* Very often people who are honestly trying to meet the conditions for healing as taught in the New Testament are defeated by forces at work in the unconscious.

> Within my earthly temple there's a crowd;
> There's one of us that's humble, one that's
>   proud;
> There's one that's broken-hearted for his sins,
> There's one that unrepentant sits and grins.[11]

Those of us who have worked steadily and conscientiously in this field of service know that one of the problems that baffle and discourage supplicants is that as far as their conscious mind is concerned they have fulfilled the essential conditions for relief but nothing has happened. We have been able to help them only as we have pointed out to them the factors at work beneath the surface that shut out God and have helped them to rid themselves of these obstacles. Some of the most remarkable healings that have taken place have followed such patient personal instruction.

4. Very important it will be *to enlist an inner group of people who are committed to this adventure,* who will take special training in the gospel of healing, will study books that are specially relevant to this phase of redemption, will be present at the services and will surround you in your ministry with loving, intelligent prayer, and will engage in intercession for those who are kneeling at the altar during your ministrations. For seven years in Mount Vernon Place Church, Baltimore, Maryland, such a group met every Wednesday for one hour in advance of the public healing service to study and pray for our adventure.

5. It seems to many of us *essential that the minister should be available for personal consultation with the persons who come for prayers.* This is not a responsibility that can be entrusted to anyone else. Often the illness is the result of tragic experiences in the past or of situations in home or work, so complicated that people not only find faith difficult but are constantly subjected to irritations and infections and indignities that aggravate their condition, set up new illnesses, and fill them with despair. They need above all things, not public prayers, but private and very intimate and skilled personal counsel. Public healing services will increase the work load of the pastor who loves the people. The services will bring in persons who

would never come unless they had been persuaded by the loving ministry in the healing service that the pastor would understand them and would have the patience to give to them the sympathetic hearing and the heartfelt care which alone can help them. Surely no shepherd of the flock will regret the new opportunity thus presented to lead people into green pastures and beside the still waters, and to restore the souls that have been all but destroyed by the turbulences of life and by the famine imposed upon their very human hungers.

6. Finally, it cannot be stressed too much that *the minister should make every effort to be informed both about the scriptures and about the findings of science in this area.* The pastor is not a scientist but a minister whose authority lies in the realm of the spirit. The minister will not attempt deep analysis unless special training has been attained. But enough should be known about what is going on in the world in which the people live that the minister will not make statements that are ridiculous and discredit the gospel and destroy confidence in the pastor's sanity. I shall never forget the time when I heard one man, who should have known better, tell his listeners that they must "get rid of the subconscious." What a piece of advice! They cannot get rid of the subconscious. They ought not to try. They will need it in the business of living. They may cleanse it but they should not waste any time trying to abolish it. Some have told their audiences that to go to a psychiatrist is turn away from Christ. Jesus said, "you shall know the truth and the truth

shall make you free." All truth is God's truth from whatever source it comes. Let us stay on God's side always.

* * * * * *

Blessings on you who are seeking to follow in the footsteps of Jesus and to fulfill his command to heal the sick in his name and through his name and through his power. Keep humble. Hold sacred the confidences entrusted to your keeping. Be patient with those who need to come again and again. Guard against the intrusions of well-meaning people who have an unenlightened zeal for God and whose too readily volunteered testimony and exhortation are the source of endless confusion. Let no current skepticisms daunt you. Not everyone will experience the specific healing he or she is seeking, but many will. However, each one will be blessed and helped in some way. Be alert to discover in the unhealed or in their environment or in yourself any hindrances to the renewal of life and seek to clear them away.

This ministry requires constant self-examination and ever larger dedication. Whatever else you do, keep on loving those who need you, those who oppose you, those who fail you. If necessary, lose your life for their sakes and for Christ. So doing you will find life for yourself and for your people on deeper levels. You are Christ's missioner and he will never fail you or your people!

APPENDIX THREE
The Disciplined Order of Christ

Under the leadership of Dr. Albert E. Day in the summer of 1945, one hundred twenty clergy and laypersons met at Albion College in Michigan to seek God's guidance at the close of World War II. Together they caught a vision of what life can be under Christ—a life of ethical sensitivity, spiritual insight, social concern, and heroic devotion to the kingdom of God. To those gathered at Albion, it seemed that nothing less than such a life revealed through Jesus Christ would be adequate for the moral confusion, personal dilemmas, and social crises of the modern world. To foster such a life, the Disciplined Order of Christ was founded.

A unique feature of the D.O.C. is the practice of these seven spiritual disciplines with an annual renewal and accountability:

1. Setting aside a daily time for private prayer, meditation, serious study of the Bible and other great religious literature.
2. Personal commitment to a lifestyle which emphasizes obedience, simplicity, humility, frugality, generosity, truthfulness, purity, and charity.
3. Participation in a small group fellowship for the sharing of insights, problems, joys, and for prayer and social action.
4. Active involvement in the ministry of an organized church.
5. Witnessing their faith to others and sharing the good news of the kingdom of God.

6. Recognition of God's gracious gifts of body, mind, spirit, and all material things, and of their obligation to use these gifts in service to others.
7. The discipline of ecumenical fellowship recognizing that all persons are worthy of Christian love.

The Disciplined Order of Christ is a spiritual movement of persons who are seriously committed to disciplines and practices required for growing in the mind and spirit of Christ.

For further information contact:

The Disciplined Order of Christ
National Headquarters
P. O. Box 189   Nashville, TN 37202

These books authored by Albert E. Day may be ordered from the national headquarters:

Discipline and Discovery (original)
Discipline and Discovery (workbook edition)
An Autobiography of Prayer
The Cup and the Sword

Notes

1. Schubert M. Ogden, *Christ Without Myth* (New York: Harper & Row, 1961), pp. 159-61.

2. Guenther Bornkamm, *Jesus of Nazareth,* translated by James M. Robinson (New York: Harper & Brothers, 1960), pp. 130-31.

3. Ruth Cranston, *The Miracle of Lourdes* (New York: McGraw Hill Book Company, 1955), pp. 60-61.

4. The seminar reports were published by Wainwright House, Miller's Point, Rye, New York (International Headquarters of The Layman's Movement).

5. Samuel H. Miller, *The Dilemma of Modern Belief* (New York: Harper & Row, 1963), p. 16.

6. "I Sought the Lord," in *The Methodist Hymnal* (Nashville: The Methodist Publishing House, 1966).

7. William Herbert Carruth, "Each in His Own Tongue," in *Each in His Own Tongue and Other Poems* (New York: G. P. Putnam's Sons, 1924).

8. James Montgomery, "At Home in Heaven."

9. Alfred Tennyson, "Strong Son of God, Immortal Love."

10. Gertrude More, "Be Thou My Chooser for Me" in *The Fellowship of the Saints,* comp. Thomas S. Kepler (New York: Abingdon-Cokesbury Press, 1963), p. 339.

11. Edward Sanford Martin, "My Name Is Legion," in *Masterpieces of Religious Verse*, ed. James Dalton Morrison (New York: Harper & Brothers, 1948), p. 274.

Albert E. Day (1884-1973) was the founder and original guiding force behind the Disciplined Order of Christ. He pastored churches in several states and held lectureships at, among other schools, Yale, Emory University, and Southern Methodist University.

Dr. Day's other books include *An Autobiography of Prayer, The Cup and the Sword,* and *Discipline and Discovery.*